Robert Mic...
Matthew V...

Colour illustrations by
Simon Schatz

Junkers Ju 87
"STUKA"

STRATUS

Published in Poland in 2008
by STRATUS s.c.
Po. Box 123,
27-600 Sandomierz 1, Poland
e-mail:office@mmpbooks.biz
for
Mushroom Model Publications,
36 Ver Road, Redbourn,
AL3 7PE, UK.
e-mail: rogerw@mmpbooks.biz

© 2008 Mushroom Model
Publications.
http://www.mmpbooks.biz

All rights reserved. Apart from any fair dealing for the purpose of private study, research, criticism or review, as permitted under the Copyright, Design and Patents Act, 1988, no part of this publication may be reproduced, stored in a retrieval system, or transmitted in any form or by any means, electronic, electrical, chemical, mechanical, optical, photocopying, recording or otherwise, without prior written permission. All enquiries should be addressed to the publisher.

**ISBN
978-83-89450-49-4**

Editor in chief
Roger Wallsgrove

Editorial Team
James Kightly
Bartłomiej Belcarz
Artur Juszczak
Robert Pęczkowski

Translation
Wojtek Matusiak

Colour Drawings
Simon Schatz
(www.rlm.at)

Scale Plans
Dariusz Karnas

DTP
Robert Pęczkowski

*Printed by:
Drukarnia Diecezjalna,
ul. Żeromskiego 4,
27-600 Sandomierz*

Contents

Introduction 3
Background 4
Ju 87 Genesis 5
The first prototypes 8
Junkers Ju 87A 14
Junkers Ju 87B 22
Junkers Ju-87 R 35
Tropical versions 38
Junkers Ju 87C 39
Junkers Ju 87D 42
Junkers Ju 87D night versions 57
Junkers Ju 87E 59
Junkers Ju 87G 60
Junkers Ju 87H 63
Uncompleted developments: Ju 87F, Ju 187 & Ju 287. . 63
Junkers Ju 87 Production 64
Technical Data 65
Detail photos 67
    Ju 87A 67
    Ju 87B 76
    Ju 87D-G 102
Colour profiles 123
Bibliography 152

Get in the picture!
Do you have photographs of historical aircraft, airfields in action, or original and unusual stories to tell?
MMP would like to hear from you! We welcome previously unpublished material that will help to make MMP books the best of their kind. We will return original photos to you and provide full credit for your images. Contact us before sending us any valuable material: rogerw@mmpbooks.biz

Acknowledgements

The authors would like to thank the following people for their help and encouragement during the preparation of this publication: Peter Arnold, Deneś Bernád. Manfred Griehl, Tomasz Kopański, Rob Leigh, Kenneth Merrick, Alfred Price, Robert Panek, Steve Tournay, Peter Smith, Mike Shreeve and Hannu Valtonen.

On the title page: Ju 87A of St.G 165, winter 1938/39.
via R. Michulec.

Introduction

The Junkers Ju 87 was one of the most critically important aircraft of the Second World War. Utterly synonymous with the devastating 'Blitzkrieg' warfare that allowed German forces to sweep across Europe, the Ju 87 is symbolic of both the zenith and the nadir of the concept of the tactical dive bomber. So iconic is the Junkers creation that the abbreviated German term for dive bomber, 'Stuka', has become a name for the Ju 87 alone. (Stuka is short for *Sturzkampfflugzeug*, literally 'dive-bombing warplane'.) The arrival of the Ju 87 was an item that also clearly signalled the intent of Hitler's Third Reich as it could not be regarded as a defensive weapon, but only one for offence. How effective it was nevertheless came as a shock in 1939, despite the knowledge of German trials and limited use in the Spanish Civil War.

The Ju 87 was employed as a form of mobile, tactically flexible artillery, closely co-operating with infantry and tank forces. Stuka units used their devastating precision to punch holes in the enemy front lines, through which ground forces would pour. The dive bombers would then hamper counter attacks and consolidate the position of the tanks and infantry. Conventional level bombing was unable to achieve adequate accuracy in these tasks partly due to the inadequacies of available bombsights and also simply the distance between release point and target. In addition, the psychological and propaganda effect of this terrifying 'super weapon' had an attested effect upon the German's enemies and a positive effect on the German ground forces' morale. In this way, Poland, and later France and Belgium were overrun in a matter of weeks in each campaign. The deadly integration of forces allowed Germany to defeat countries with equipment that was no worse. It was the Stuka, with its pinpoint precision and howling dive-brakes and siren, that characterised Blitzkrieg. However, when used outside its tactical niche, and without adequate air-superiority, the Ju 87 proved vulnerable. In the Battle of Britain, after a successful campaign against Channel shipping, where the *Luftwaffe* tried to use the Stuka in a strategic role for which it was neither intended or crews were trained, it suffered unsustainable losses and was partly withdrawn. Later, in the Mediterranean and the Eastern Front, the Stuka regained its fearsome reputation.

Ju 87B under a camouflage net, France 1940.
Stratus coll.

Background

Prof. Hugo Junkers.
(3 February 1859
– 3 February 1935)
via R. Michulec

The dive bomber was not a German invention, but it was certainly Germany that developed the concept of land-based dive bombers to its fullest and used it most effectively. From 1917 to 1919, the British undertook the first major quantified trials of dive-bombing, at Orfordness, Suffolk, but with the restrictions of post-W.W.I aviation, this experiment was abandoned and forgotten. Officials in the nascent *Luftwaffe* became impressed with the development of dive bombing by the US Navy, and certain factions in the German government lobbied strongly for this type of aircraft, while others resisted the move to develop dive bombing. Other schools of thought included General Walter Wever who favoured developing large aircraft for strategic bombing (but whose death halted this aspect of the *Luftwaffe*'s development) while General Wolfram Freiherr von Richthofen believed that tactical, 'battlefield', air warfare should be carried out by low flying ground-attack aircraft. Von Richtofen's views were partly based on the developments in anti-aircraft guns in Germany at the time, which would prove to be more effective, and more effectively implemented, than Allied equivalents at the time. This led von Richtofen to suggest that a dive bomber, which must hold a fixed course at a relatively low speed to deliver its bombs accurately, would be too vulnerable to anti-aircraft fire. He thought the solution was fast, low-level attacks which would sacrifice some accuracy for a greatly reduced rate of loss.

Unlike in the UK and France, the 'dive bombing' lobby was successful in making this form of warfare a significant part of *Luftwaffe* policy. There were also technical factors in this political victory - the RLM was struggling to develop the ability to bomb accurately from altitude. The standard bomb sight available for level bombing in German aircraft in the 1930s was the Gearz-Visier 219, which could not be used above 3,000m altitude (9,900ft) and even then was not precise enough to guarantee hitting a target any smaller than a town. The results of this were graphically demonstrated in the attack on Guernica in the Spanish Civil War, in which the Legion Kondor levelled the town while attempting to destroy a bridge. The American experience, along with later trials, showed that dive bombing could offer considerably greater accuracy, enough to successfully attack targets such as ships, columns of tanks or road junctions, although with potentially higher losses than a level-bombing attack from medium altitude.

Another consideration that led to the development of dive bombing in the resurgent German air force was cost and the need to quickly build large numbers of aircraft. The Versailles Treaty had severely limited German forces and their equipment since the end of the First World War. When the Nazi government wished to rearm, it was starting from a lower base in terms of men, machinery and knowledge than its European counterparts. Single or two-seat dive-bombers were technically simpler than larger aircraft and easier to produce in volume. Cost was another consideration - at 131,000 Reichsmarks, the *Luftwaffe* could have nearly two Ju 87s for every medium bomber, for instance the Dornier Do17Z which cost RM 235,000 in 1941 prices.

Ju 87 Genesis

The first origins of what would lead to the Junkers Ju 87 date back to 1927 when the Turkish government commissioned Junkers to construct a fast, modern single or two-seat aircraft. Karl Plauth designed a cantilever monoplane with fixed undercarriage and a twin tail. In a break with recent Junkers designs, the A48 had a smooth-skinned fuselage, while the flying surfaces retained the typical Junkers corrugated skin. Technically a civil aircraft for sports and training use, the designer's intentions for possible military applications were apparent. A number of aircraft were constructed and trialled with various different radial engines and several were also constructed by AB Flygindustri, a subsidiary of Junkers, at Malmö near Limhamn in Sweden. Turkey had by now lost interest in the A48 as a fighter bomber, but its inherent strength made it an obvious candidate for dive bombing with under-wing rack mounted bombs. Plauth died before he saw his creation fly but his design team carried on the work. (Some sources claim that after the designer's death the A48/K47 was given the name "Plauth".)

At the same time as military trials of the A48 (with rocket projectiles) were taking place at Frösön, the Swedish air force was testing dive bombing with its licence-built Hawker Harts and this quite possibly further influenced the German air force's interest in dive bombing. Later tests on the A48 included specialised air-brakes, bomb sight and automatic pull-out device for use in diving attacks.

Extensive trials were carried out with the Junkers A48 in this form of attack in Sweden and the Soviet Union, including attacks on a mock-up of a ship. The technique of diving from an altitude of 3,000m (9,900ft) at a 70° angle, and releasing the bombs at between 1,000m (3,300ft) and 800m (2,600ft) was developed, and this achieved a success rate of 60% hits on target. While testing in Sweden was supervised by the Swedish military, the tests at the jointly established German-Soviet training establishment at Lipetsk in the Soviet Union gave the German military more freedom to manage their own affairs with growing confidence. (Due to the end of the joint German-Soviet programme, both aircraft returned to Germany in July 1933. With the shutdown of the school at Lipetsk in the spring, it seems that the tests referred to above could only have been be carried out in 1932.)

Junkers K47, a two seat fighter version of the A48.
via R. Michulec

Side view of K48, W.Nr. 3365 with civil registration D-2012. The example shown is powered by a Siemens Sh 20 engine.
via R. Michulec.

Tests of the A48 lasted until 1933 and undoubtedly taught Junkers a vast amount about producing a successful dive bomber. During this period, a gradual shift in the international political situation gave German manufacturers more freedom to develop military aircraft. The calculated erosion of Versailles Treaty terms by Germany accompanied a more acquiescent attitude among European powers to German rearmament in the late 1920s and early 1930s. Overseas orders for German manufacturers undoubtedly enabled greater freedom to advance the technology of military aviation, and it was an order such as this that led to the Heinkel He 50, regarded as the first true dive bomber of German design and manufacture.

The Imperial Japanese Navy had, like many armed forces around the world, become impressed with the possibilities offered by dive bombing, and commissioned Heinkel to develop such an aircraft to rival US designs such as the Curtiss F8C 'Helldiver'. Heinkel designed a two-seat biplane of mixed wood and steel tube construction powered by a licence-built Jupiter radial. The terms of the agreement were finalised in 1930, and the following year the prototype Heinkel He 50 flew. The IJN secured the rights to build the aircraft as the Aichi D1A. A second prototype was exhibited for the German armed services in 1932, and this type impressed the German government enough to order 60 in 1933 split between Heinkel and Bayerische Flugzeugwerke (later Messerschmitt) with another 12, ordered by China, later retained by the *Luftwaffe*. This aircraft equipped ten units and was the basis of *Luftwaffe* dive bombing. It was later

He 50A, the first purpose-built German dive bomber.
via R. Michulec.

used as a trainer and saw service in the Second World War as a 'night harassment' aircraft on the Eastern Front.

The He 50 confirmed the place of the dive bomber within the armoury of the German air forces. The development of a more modern aircraft to take this form of warfare to the next level was initiated by the German Air Ministry in 1934. Despite the growing confidence in dive bombing, the ministry was still undecided as to the best form the aircraft should take, either a larger aircraft capable of carrying heavier bombs, or a simpler and lighter single seater with lower payload. As a result, two development programmes were announced, the *Sofortprogramm* for a 'light Stuka' and a corresponding programme for a heavy, two seat dive bomber, the *Sturzbomber*. The former programme was initiated partly because it was expected that the smaller aircraft could be in service more quickly than the two-seater, which meant that with the latter programme, more emphasis could be given to designing a state-of-the-art aircraft. Following winter exercises in 1933-4 it was also believed that there could be a place in the battle scheme for two types - a tactical aircraft for ground attack with a secondary fighter role, and a heavier and more capable aircraft for attacking more substantial targets. This aircraft was intended to paralyse enemy infantry and tank forces, destroy artillery and prevent opposition to German ground forces from having any effect. It required armour and a rear gunner for defence against fighter attack while the light dive bomber could rely on its greater agility for survival.

The first programme resulted in the the Fieseler Fi 98 and Henschel Hs 123, which were both single-seat biplanes powered by a BMW radial. The prototypes first flew in 1935 and the Henschel was selected. The small biplane was capable of carrying out steep diving attacks with an armament of four 50kg (110lb) bombs, enough to knock out a light tank or soft-skinned targets. It was extremely tough and saw a good deal of action in the Spanish Civil War and the Second World War in the ground attack role.

The more important heavy dive bomber programme was formally announced in January 1935. This was in fact drawn up around proposals that had been made to the RLM following Junkers' experiences with the A48, and the company had already been awarded a contract for three prototypes. The Ju 87 was born.

Hs 123 V2, D-ILUA, the second prototype of the light "Stuka".

via R. Michulec.

The first prototypes

The first prototype of the Junkers dive bomber, designated Ju 87 V1 (W.Nr. 4921) was built at Dessau, and was ready by April 1935. It employed most of the experience built up through the years of testing and trials, and the early use of dive bombers in the German air arm - which became the *Luftwaffe* in 1935. The single-engined monoplane shared the twin-tail, low-wing monoplane layout of the A48, but there the similarity ended. The engine was a liquid cooled in-line unit - a Rolls Royce Kestrel V when the V1 was built - rather than the A48's radial. The fixed undercarriage was faired by substantial trousers, needed to cover the forward-leaning oleo-legs and struts carried aft to stabilise the unit. Small struts also braced the undercarriage to the fuselage underside. The crew were housed in an extensively glazed cockpit with good vision all round. The most distinctive feature was the wing, with its inverted-gull profile and slotted ailerons and flaps. The aircraft was of all-metal, stressed-skin construction with the emphasis very much on strength.

Junkers spent several months resolving minor problems with the new aircraft until it was ready for flight on the 17th September 1935 at the hands of Willi Neuenhofen. The first flights revealed a lack of stability and inefficient engine cooling. Junkers sought to resolve the latter issue by installing a larger radiator, canted within the fuselage to retain a smaller frontal area. This also proved insufficient, so the radiator was fitted vertically and the intake deepened, giving the characteristic 'beard' profile. In December 1935, with only one prototype flying and before the state trials for a new dive bomber, the RLM contracted Junkers to build 11 pre-production aircraft in addition to the prototypes.

Many further flights took place, including diving tests even though the specially designed airbrakes were not ready. During one of these dives, at 60°, on the 24th January 1936, the starboard fin ripped off leading to an uncontrollable spin. The Ju 87 V1 hit the ground, killing Neuenhofen and his observer. As a result of this, the Ju 87 Versuch 2 (V2 - W.Nr. 4922 registration D-UHUH), which

The Ju 87 V1, W.Nr. 4921, in its original form, just before the maiden flight on 17th September 1935. via R. Michulec.

had been completed in November 1935, was rebuilt. The crash was traced to insufficient structural strength in the tail for the stresses of diving and recovery. The twin fins, included to provide an excellent field of fire for the rear gunner, were therefore replaced with a large single fin and redesigned tail plane. The dive brakes, a slotted plate underneath each wing which swivelled 90° until perpendicular to the airflow, were also added to ensure that the speed in dives was limited and therefore avoid overstressing the structures.

During the rebuild, the Ju 87 V2's Rolls Royce engine was replaced with a Junkers Jumo 210A 610 which delivered 610 PS (600 hp) and was more representative of the production standard powerplant. The two-bladed, fixed-pitch propeller was also replaced with a three-bladed variable-pitch Hamilton

Another photo of the Ju 87 V1, W.Nr. 4921.

via R. Michulec.

The Ju 87 V1 with a new, larger, radiator and modified cowlings.

via R. Michulec.

Junkers Ju 87 "STUKA"

Ju 87 V3, W.Nr. 4923, D-UKYQ, in flight.
via R. Michulec.

Standard unit licence built by Junkers. This version was the first to fly with armament, as a machine gun was carried in the rear cockpit.

The first flight of the rebuilt Ju 87 V2 took place on the 25th February 1936. Further work was carried out on the tail unit, including the addition of struts under the tail planes and the replacement of the rudder with a larger item.

Meanwhile the third prototype, the Ju 87 V3, D-UKYQ, had been completed and flew on the 27th March 1936. This airframe included all the improvements that had been made to the V2, and it was this aircraft that would take part in the *Luftwaffe*'s trials to select a new dive bomber. These trials almost never took place, as Wolfram von Richthofen cancelled the dive bomber programme in June 1936. However, von Richthofen was soon replaced by the dive bomber's biggest advocate, Ernst Udet, who reinstated the programme and the trials.

The trials took place at Rechlin in June 1936, and pitted the Junkers against three other aircraft.

To a degree, the Junkers had always been the favourite to win selection for the *Luftwaffe*. The programme itself had resulted from Junkers' experiences, and the manufacturer had the experience of the A48 programme. However, the Ju 87's success was by no means a foregone conclusion. Its competitors included an entry by Heinkel, which had provided the *Luftwaffe*'s first dive bomber, and aircraft from Arado and Blohm & Voss.

The Arado Ar 81 was the least modern of the entrants. It was the only biplane, with slightly swept wings of equal span. It had a narrow boom rear fuselage and its braced tail had twin fins to give the best possible field of fire and visibility for the rear gunner, and fixed, spatted undercarriage. It was powered by a Jumo 210C liquid cooled engine and had a variable-pitch propeller.

The Blohm & Voss Ha 137 was another of the more unlikely contenders. It was not designed specifically to meet the Sturzbomber programme but was initially intended to trial design concepts developed by designer Richard Vogt. It carried a single crew member in an open cockpit while the requirement called for a two-seat aircraft. The Ha 137 was, however, the closest in layout to the Ju 87. It was an all-metal monoplane with a heavily cranked wing built according to Vogt's tube-spar principle, with the spar also forming the main fuel tank. It featured fixed, trousered undercarriage at the dihedral break with the inverted gull wing making for very short oleo legs. It was otherwise conventional, and initially powered by a licence built Pratt & Whitney Hornet radial, which later changed to a Junkers Jumo in-line engine. As a dive bomber it gave a great deal away to the other competitors as it could only carry smaller bombs which were fitted in racks beneath the wings rather than on the centreline. Its presence at the trials had much to do with von Richthofen's continued influence, as the Ha 137 showed potential in the ground attack role he favoured, especially with the 20mm cannon it was designed to carry.

The Ju 87's biggest threat came from Heinkel, which had entered the He 118. This aircraft was the most modern and aerodynamically clean of all the entrants. It boasted retractable undercarriage, a semi-elliptical wing and internal bomb carriage. The efficient design owed much to the company's experience with the He112 fighter and the He 70 fast mailplane, to both of which the He118 bore a family resemblance.

Like the Junkers, the Heinkel started life with a Rolls Royce engine, in this case a Buzzard rated at 845hp (62.6kW). The intended powerplant was a Daimler Benz DB600, and when this was fitted, it was claimed that the Heinkel reached speeds in excess of 270mph (434kph). This was considerably higher than any of the other competitors.

The Blohm & Voss and Arado entries were quickly discounted despite the latter's impressive dive bombing performance during the tests - its outmoded layout was simply no match for the state-of-the-art monoplanes. The Heinkel was a thoroughly modern aircraft and the best performing of the four, but in dive bombing tests it proved inferior to the Junkers. The He 118 had a complicated system of air-brakes which were connected to the propeller pitch which

Side view of Ju 87 V3, W.Nr. 4923, in flight.
via R. Michulec.

Heinkel were struggling to perfect, and the test pilots were unable to push the aircraft to dive at more than 50° to the horizontal which was insufficient for an accurate dive bombing attack. Meanwhile the Ju 87 was able to achieve near-vertical dives for pin-point accuracy.

The trials were virtually decided in Junkers' favour when Udet decided to try the He 118 himself. He failed to comprehend the complicated airbrake-propeller link and entered the dive with the propeller in the wrong pitch. The reduction gear flew off and the aircraft broke up in mid-air. Udet bailed out, and by the time he reached the ground, the success of the Ju 87 was effectively guaranteed.

Junkers engineers at Dessau had not been idle during the competition, and had worked hard on the Ju 87V4 (W.Nr. 4924, civil registration D-UBIP). It flew on the 20th June 1936 and was largely production-standard. The machine introduced a number of innovations in order to improve crew operating conditions and to reinforce the structure. The engine mount was lowered by 10 in producing a sloping nose profile, which aided forward visibility, the aft fuselage was reinforced, the rear canopy was modified and a window was fitted in the cockpit floor to allow easier target identification by the pilot. The tail fin and rudder were further increased in height and area, and made more square in profile with a less-swept leading edge. Full military equipment was fitted to the Ju 87 V4 including a dedicated dive-bombing version of the Revi C/12A sight (known informally as Stuvi), a new bomb rack installation (Schloß 500 XIB) and modified bomb release arm to swing the main bomb clear of the propeller arc. The standard bomb load was 250 kg (550 lb) but more could be carried if the observer was left on the ground.

Ju 87 V4, W.Nr. 4924, D–UBIP was a production-standard prototype for the Ju 87A.
via R. Michulec.

In September 1936 the aircraft was sent for state tests to Rechlin, which continued until January 1937. Final refinements were requested such as small alterations of the wing tip and leading edge to simplify production. The engine had to be replaced with a more powerful one, as with the Jumo 210A the machine could barely carry a 500 kg bomb and only when flown without the second crew member so a Jumo 210C was specified.

Side view of the Ju 87 V4.
via R. Michulec.

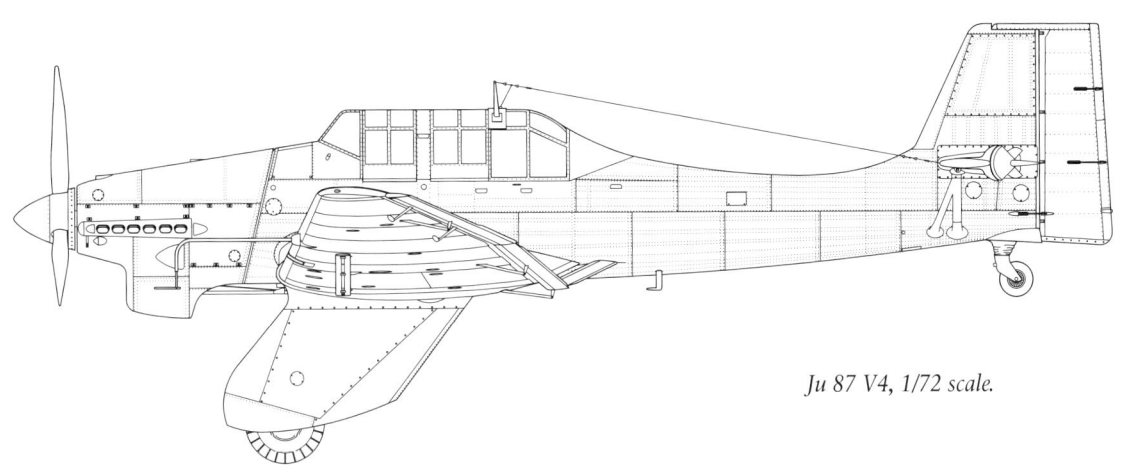

Ju 87 V4, 1/72 scale.

Junkers Ju 87 A

In November 1935 the Dessau factory started assembly of another prototype, the Ju 87 V5, (W.Nr. 4925) which was flown on 14th August 1936. This was the pattern aircraft for the production Ju 87 A (popularly known as the 'Anton') with full armament and equipment. Even at this stage in proceedings, thought was given to changing the powerplant to the Daimler-Benz DB600 which had impressed in the Heinkel He 118. However, the Junkers Jumo was retained and the V5 was fitted with a Jumo 210C (itself to be later replaced with a more powerful development, the Jumo 210D). The Ju 87 V5 was dispatched to Rechlin where it spent the rest of 1936 engaged in testing.

Even as the Ju 87 V5 was completed, Junkers was preparing for the construction of eleven pre-production aircraft for extensive pre-service testing that the RLM had requested back in December 1935. In August 1936 the aircraft, now designated Ju 87A-0, were begun with the serials W.Nr. 0001 to 0011. Like all the Ju 87s so far, they were civillian registered, and bore the registrations D-IEAA to D-IEAK. Between April and July 1937 the A-0 series Ju 87s began field trials, possibly with by I./StG 162 "Immelman", and during this time it is likely they gained military markings and serials. Like the V4 they were powered by the Jumo 210C and carried full military equipment.

At Dessau, preparations for series production of the A-1 series variant started in early 1937, while the A-0 series was under construction. The first true production Ju 87s did not differ significantly from the pre-production batch but changes were made on the production line from November 1937. These included rounding off the upper rear corner of the rudder, upgrading the powerplant to the Jumo 210D and fitment of a more modern radio set, the FuG VII. These improved machines were designated Ju 87A-2. For a time, production of Ju 87A-1s continued alongside the A-2 with the earlier model being built until summer 1938. One of the first Ju 87A-1s, W.Nr. 0013 (carrying civil registration D-ILGM) was taken from the production line to confirm that the production Ju 87 was of suitable quality.

The first, production, Ju 87A-1, W.Nr. 0012, D–IEAU, built at the Dessau factory in 1936. The last two digits of the W.Nr. were painted under the horizontal tailplane.

via R. Michulec.

Though it seems quality was satisfactory, the RLM desired that the new dive bomber should be produced at a greater rate than Junkers could achieve - during 1937 only 121 Ju 87s were completed by the company[1]. The RLM had in fact arranged for Weserflug[2] at Lemwerder, near Bremen, to licence build the

Ju 87A of KG 157, 1938. Note that tactical number is painted under the wings as well as on the fuselage.
via R. Michulec.

---

1 According to Junkers data 144 Ju 87s were built in 1937, including 3 prototypes and 11 machines in the A-0 batch. This would mean that 130 production machines were completed. It is possible that the difference between 121 and 130 was due to omitting the two K-1 aircraft despatched to Japan and three A-1s sent to Spain. Four machines would still be missing, however. Possibly the difference between 'started' and 'finished' airframes could account for the variation, or parts made by subcontractors but not yet completed. (Data in the text based on RLM listings.)

2 Weserflug, short for "Weser" Flugzeugbau GmbH (abbreviated WFG).

A line of Ju 87As of StG 165 at an auxiliary airfield in summer 1938.
via T. Kopański.

aircraft during 1936 in case the volume of production needed to be increased and this was put into action with *Lieferplan* (Delivery Schedule) 5 in April 1937. In October of that year, Weserflug began constructing Ju 87A -models from sub-assemblies and components provided by Junkers and contractor companies. In October 1937, two Stukas were completed, a further five by the beginning of 1938 and a further five were ready by the end of March 1938 including the first machine built entirely by Weserflug, which was sent to Junkers for quality control trials.

Weserflug initially concentrated on final assembly, but took on more manufacturing of the basic Ju 87Components throughout the first half of 1938 until August 1938 when the company completed the last of the 70 Ju 87A-1s it had contracted to build. Apart from the VDM propeller in place of the Junkers-Hamilton unit on parent company-built aircraft, the Weserflug Ju 87s were identical to the original Ju 87A. Altogether, until the end of Ju 87A production, both plants built 141 aircraft, including 71 by Junkers at Dessau and 70 by Weserflug at Bremen, with 262 Ju 87A (192 of them from Junkers) built over 17 months.

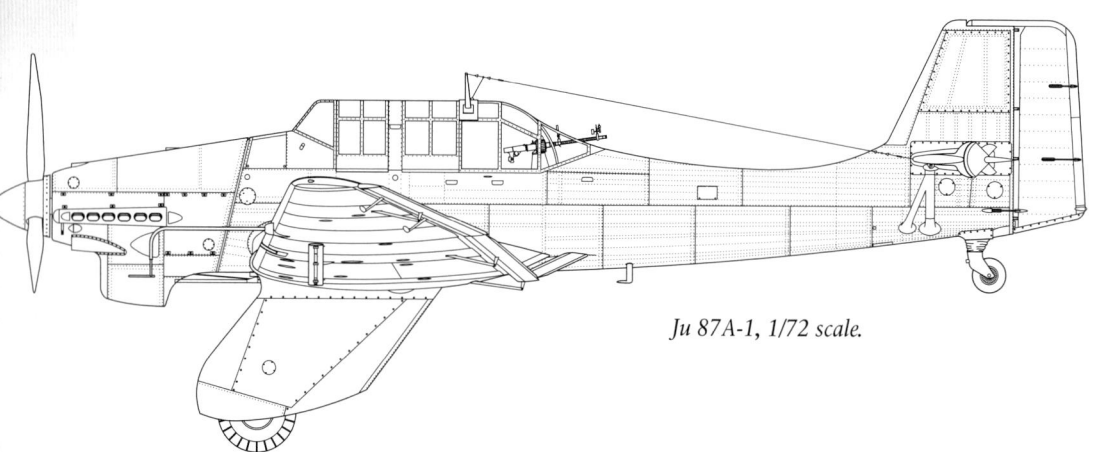

Ju 87A-1, 1/72 scale.

Bottom: A line of Ju 87As in summer 1938.
Stratus coll.

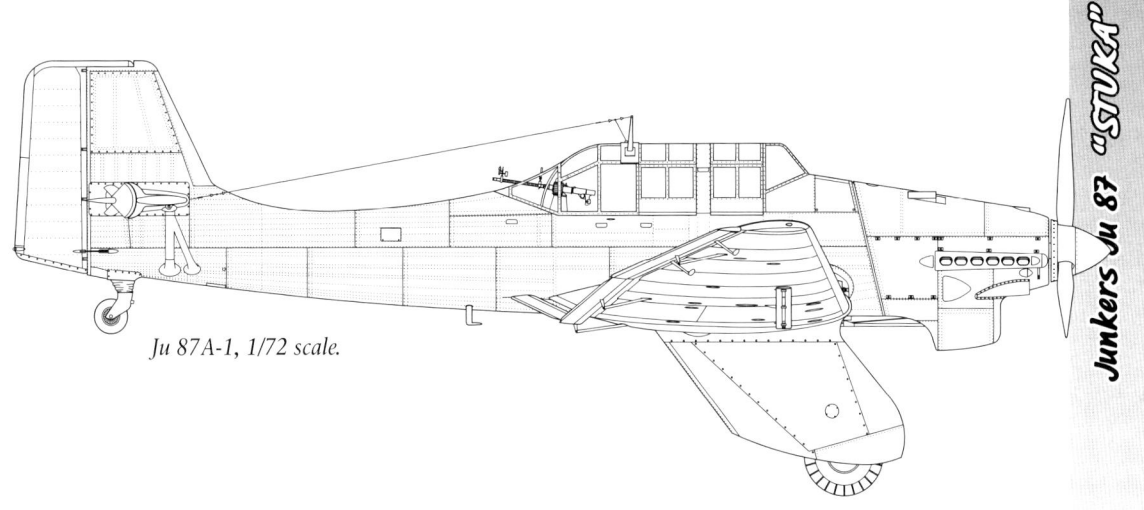

Ju 87A-1, 1/72 scale.

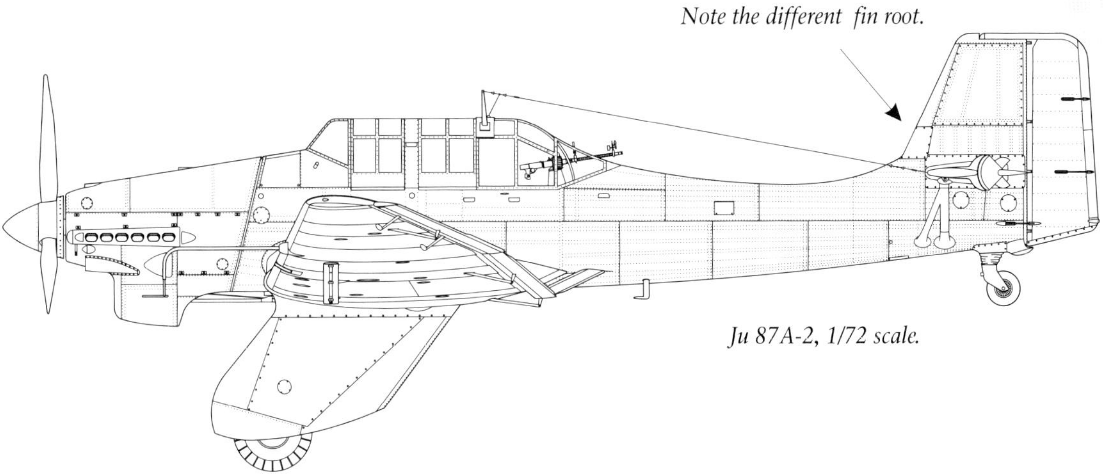

Note the different fin root.

Ju 87A-2, 1/72 scale.

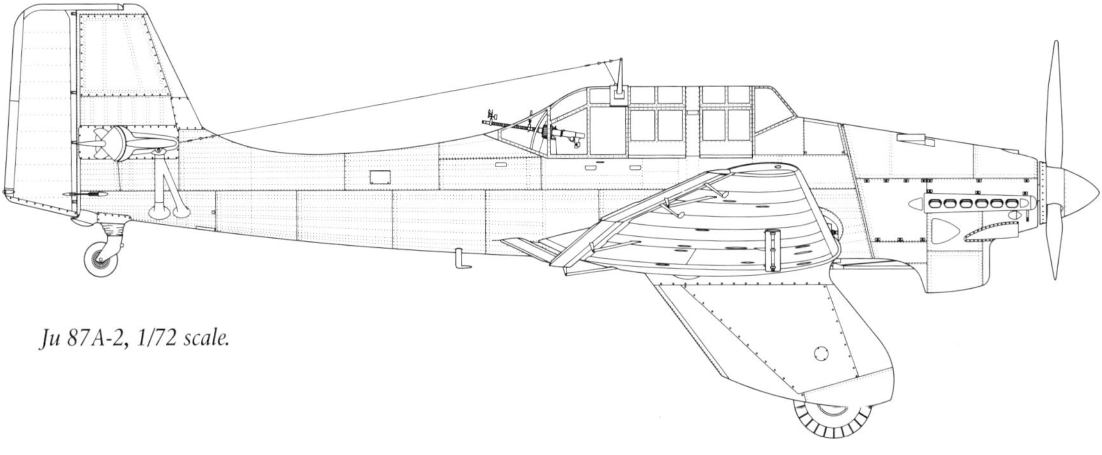

Ju 87A-2, 1/72 scale.

17

Junkers Ju 87 "STUKA"

Ju 87A-2, 1/72 scale.

Ju 87A-2 in Berlin, on display during "Wehrmacht Day", March 1939. Note that the aircraft has the new two-tone (RLM 70/RLM 71) upper surface camouflage. via R. Michulec.

Three Ju 87A-2s of StG 165, in 1938 in flight. Note the variations in the standard three tone camouflage usually obtained by switching the basic colours and splinter pattern.
                    Stratus coll.

Above: *Ju 87A-2, 1938.*
Stratus coll.

Right: *Ju 87A-1, W.Nr. 5040, built at the Weser factory in 1937, winter 1941/42. Note the wheel spats have been partially removed.*
via R. Michulec.

Ju 87A-2 of Stukakampfflieger-Schule 2, at Graz-Thalerhof.
Stratus coll.

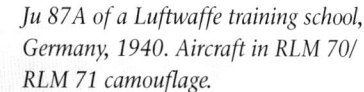

Ju 87A of a Luftwaffe training school, Germany, 1940. Aircraft in RLM 70/RLM 71 camouflage.

Ilmailumuseo.

Left: Ju 87A of Luftnachrichtenschule 5 at Erfurt-Bindersleben circa 1941.

Ilmailumuseo.

Ju 87A 29 • 4 of the Legion Condor left at a Spanish air base after the Spanish Civil War. Note that the radio installation and armament have been removed.

Ilmailumuseo..

Junkers Ju 87B

Ju 87A production had not long been underway when thought was given to improving on the initial production model. An aircraft from the initial Junkers production batch was used to test the feasibility of carrying four 50kg (110lb) bombs on wing-mounted racks. The ETC bomb carriers were fitted aft of the airbrakes under each wing for this purpose, but the Ju 87A's structure was not sufficiently strong to carry the extra weight. It is unclear whether the tests were intended to add further offensive load to the Ju 87A or as a precursor to a later, more heavily armed variant. Indeed, the trial aircraft was W.Nr. 0005, which was later recorded as testing equipment for what became the Ju 87B.

Successful though the Ju 87A was, there were undoubtedly improvements that could be made. The most obvious of these was to add more power, in the shape of the Jumo 211A which offered 1,100 PS (1,085hp), which would give greater speed and lifting ability. Indeed, the Ju 87B was some 60 km/h (33 mph) faster than its predecessor. More importantly, with only a small reduction in range, the Ju 87B could carry 700 kg (1,540 lb) of bombs. This was more than double the load of the Ju 87A. The 211A developed maximum take-off power of 1,100 PS (1,085 hp) at 2,400 rpm, and achieved its maximum combat rating at an altitude of 4,000m (13,000ft). The slightly developed 211A-1 produced 80 PS (85 hp) more and had a maximum combat rating some 500m (1,625 ft) higher.

A great propaganda head on shot of a Ju 87 B-1. The asymmetric upper cowling intake is clearly shown.

via R. Michulec.

There were a number of other significant changes to the Ju 87B, the most externally obvious being the undercarriage. Gone were the bulky trousers of the earlier models, replaced by much neater spats. This was made possible by considerable simplification and strengthening of the undercarriage itself, which was now a single oleo-leg per unit carrying the wheel on a fork, with no need for supporting struts as with the Ju 87A. The mounting point at the dihedral break was strengthened, and a spring shock absorber added in addition to the oleo-pneumatic item carried over from the Ju 87A. This lengthened the travel and raised the height of the aircraft slightly when at rest. It was a particularly neat solution, especially given that the undercarriage of the B-model had to carry more weight than the A-model.

The Jumo 211A was not only more powerful than the 210 series, it was heavier by up to 200 kg (440 lb) depending on the precise model. It was also larger - 268mm longer, 100mm taller and 118 mm wider than the older engine. This required completely new mountings, fittings and cowling panels. The 211A was also thirstier than the 210C so the Ju 87 required larger fuel tanks, but the 40

litres that were added still resulted in a lower range for the newer aircraft, with a range of 600 km as opposed to 800 km for the A models.

Installation of the Jumo 211 was similar to that of the 210, but the opportunity was taken to make some improvements to the placement of ancillary equipment. The oil cooler was relocated from below the engine to above and to port, while the carburettor intake was moved from the top of the engine to the starboard cowling. The layout of cables and fittings was revised to give much improved access. The various changes to the engine and nose profiling led to the Ju 87B gaining 300mm in length over the Ju 87A. This, and the extra weight of the Ju 87B moved the centre of gravity slightly forward, which

Ju 87 V9, W.Nr. 4927, D–IELZ, the prototype the Ju 87B-1. This aircraft was one of the few Ju 87Bs to wear three-tone camouflage.
K. Merrick.

Ju 87B-1 (early) crashed somewhere in Germany. Note the blanked off wing gun.
Stratus coll.

allowed the aircraft to nose over into the dive more easily, though it did lead to an increased number of landing and taxiing accidents where the aircraft tipped up onto its nose more readily. Flying characteristics were largely unchanged, and the Ju 87B was found to be easy and pleasant to fly with well harmonised controls and good response.

There were improvements internally as well. The cockpit was completely remodelled to improve crew comfort and safety, and the canopy was redesigned to improve visibility still further. The canopy was made up of four sections, including sliding hoods for pilot and gunner. The rearmost glazing incorporated an Ikaria spherical mount for an MG 15 machine gun, which offered a large improvement in field of fire over the Ju 87A which relied on a slot cut in the canopy - the angle to which the gun would traverse to the sides increased from 15° to 45°.

The Ju 87A had only a single forward firing machine gun, in the port wing, but on the Ju 87B a second MG 17 was added in the starboard wing. To aim these guns an improved gunsight, the Revi C/12C (known colloquially as 'Stuvi A2') was fitted, which doubled as a sight for dive bombing. The radio set fitted, which was operated by the gunner, was upgraded to the FuG VIIa.

Ju 87B-1 (early). 1/72 scale.

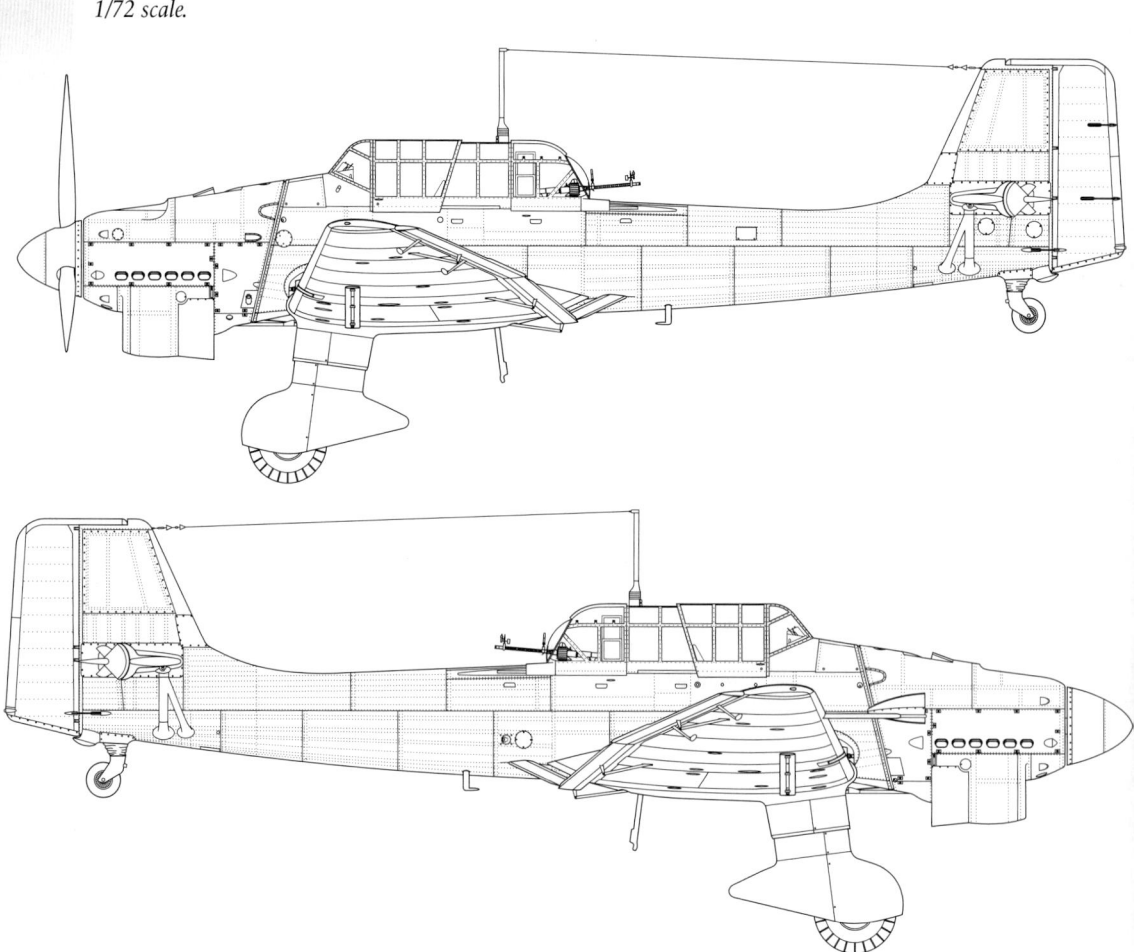

Two Ju 87B-1s of the Legion Condor, ready for the next mission in Spain. Summer, 1938.
via R. Michulec.

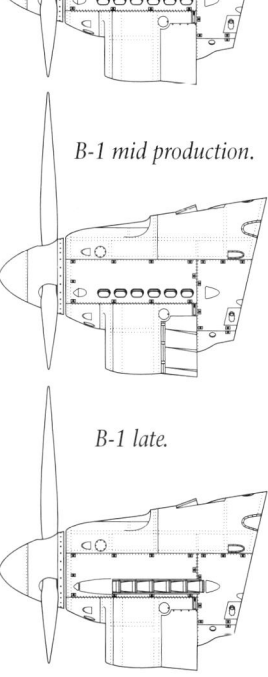

B-1 early.

B-1 mid production.

B-1 late.

Four prototypes were produced, which undertook extensive trials for the considerably improved Stuka. Further to these machines, a short run of pre-production Ju 87Bs was also built, following which the production lines of Junkers at Dessau and Weserflug at Bremen turned out their first B model Ju 87s in March and April 1938 respectively. This first production type was designated Ju 87B-1, although the Junkers and Weserflug aircraft differed slightly, most notably in the contours of the radiator cowling. By the end of 1938, both factories had built 76 of this variant, and by the end of the following year a further 525 had come off the production lines. (Unfortunately, the exact number of Ju 87B-0 built is not certain. It seems that the last A-2 could be W.Nr. 192, and the lowest Ju 87B-1 serial number was W.Nr. 198. This would suggest that the pre-production Ju 87B batch was limited to 2-5 examples.)

During the B-1's production run, an improved exhaust manifold was introduced and machines produced to this specification were designated Ju 87B-1/UI. The machines received W.Nr. serials in continuous number blocks - those from the Dessau factory had numbers from about W.Nr. 0195 to 0500 (the initial zero was often omitted when applying the serials on aircraft), and those from Bremen had W.Nr. 5072 to 5599.

In around May-June 1940, a revised B model was introduced to the Stuka production lines. Changes included an improved Jumo engine, the 211D, which offered 1,200 PS (1,185 hp), 100 PS (100 hp) more than the earlier 211A. The new powerplant was 24mm longer and 9mm deeper than the 211A. The new engine also drove a different propeller, the VS 5, which used broad-chord wooden blades as opposed to the narrower metal blades fitted to the previous VDM unit. The new engine also required a deeper radiator and slightly reprofiled cowling. Further improvements were made to the undercarriage, including a longer oleo-leg and larger (815x290 mm) tyres.

Ju 87B-1, early, France 1940.
Stratus coll.

The new Ju-87 was known as the B-2 and 225 were built at both Weserflug and Junkers until production moved to the next model in the autumn of that year. Werk numbers ranged from approximately 5550 to 6000 at "Weser", and from 0510 to 0560 at Junkers.

It appears that some Ju-87 B-1s were fitted with the Jumo 211D during routine maintenance and overhaul, bringing them closer to the B-2 standard machines[1]. Both B-1s and B-2s were also subjected to a continuous improvement programme with the use of 'Umbausatz' (conversion) kits. These resulted in three sub-variants, the U2, U3 and U4. The first of these covered various improved radio fits. In addition, this included replacement of the EiV Ia intercom with

A Ju 87B-1, late version, of Stab III./St.G 77. The upper camouflage pattern is clearly visible.
via R. Michulec.

1 It is often claimed that the aircraft were fitted with the Jumo 211 Da engines, but this is not confirmed. The same applies to similar information about other engines with the "a" suffix used in earlier Ju 87 versions.

the EiV V unit. The FuG VII radio, which required a towed aerial and Morane mast, was replaced with the PeilG IV which was itself later modified with the EZ 4 receiver, and finally the FuG 25 IFF.

The U3 modification introduced cockpit armour. The U4 designation was given to aircraft fitted with ski-undercarriage, which was tested in Estonia in the winter of 1941-42 and 1942-43.

The Ju 87B's entry into service was marred by a bizarre and tragic incident at a demonstration for *Luftwaffe* leaders on the eve of war. Three staffeln of Ju 87s were to dive bomb a target at Neuhammer with smoke bombs, which they had to do by plunging through a forecast two layers of cloud. However, as the Stukas were on their way to the target, one layer of cloud had dissipated, while a ground mist had formed. Mistaking the mist for cloud, thirteen of the Stukas plunged straight into the ground. Weeks later, the survivors and their aircraft were at war in Poland.

The Ju 87B 'Berta' was the major type of Stuka in *Luftwaffe* service at the beginning of the Second World War, and contributed hugely to the German domination of Europe. However, when Ju 87s were required to operate without air superiority and with objectives other than their traditional battlefield targets, during the Battle of Britain, the Stuka suffered considerable losses, due to the lack of *Luftwaffe* air superiority. Some squadrons sustained heavy losses before the Ju 87 units were partly withdrawn from the battle.

A pair of Ju 87B-1s of I./St.G 2, France 1940.
via R. Michulec.

Above: Ju 87B-2 of Stab III./St.G 77, ready for a mission against Crete, May, 1941. *via A. Price.*
Below: Ju 87B-1 built by JFM Dessau, unknown training unit, 1941. *via R. Michulec.*

Ju 87R about to take off from a desert airstrip.
            via R. Michulec.

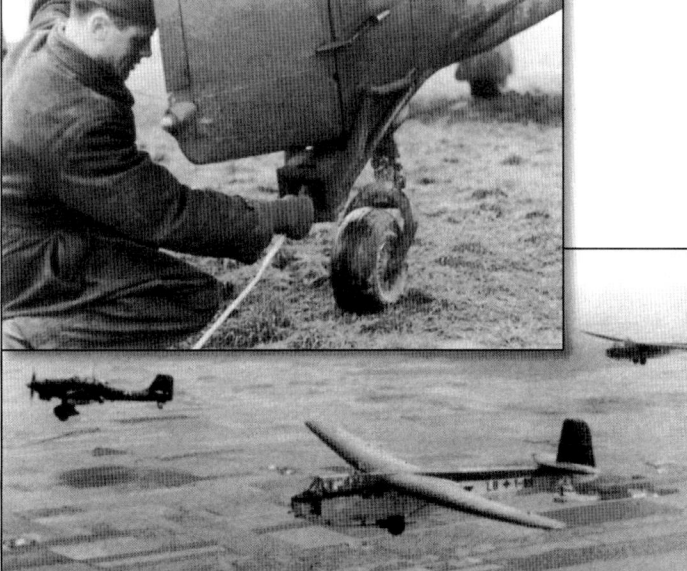

Left: *Ju 87B with tail-box attachment for glider towing.*
            via R. Michulec.

Left, Bottom: *Ju 87R-2 as a glider tug.*
            via R. Michulec.

Below: *Ju 87B-1 of St.G 2 at Lyon, France, June 1940.*
            Stratus coll.

Junkers Ju 87 "STUKA"

Ju 87 B-2. 1/72 scale.
Note the Jericho-Trompete *(Trumpets of Jericho)* wind-driven sirens sometimes fitted to the undercarriage legs as shown here. These were for (highly effective) psychological warfare but caused significant drag, leading to their removal.
1/72 scale.

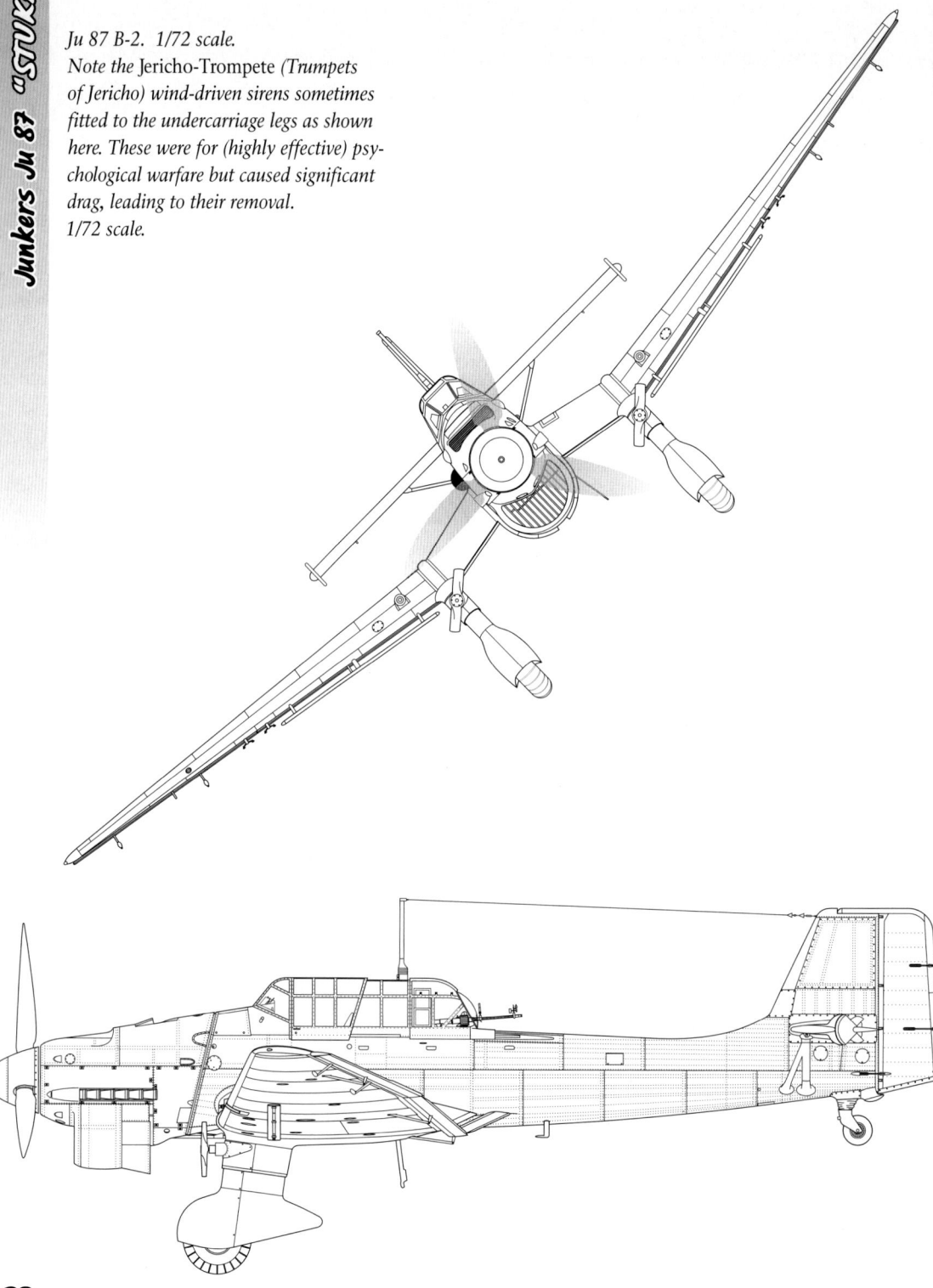

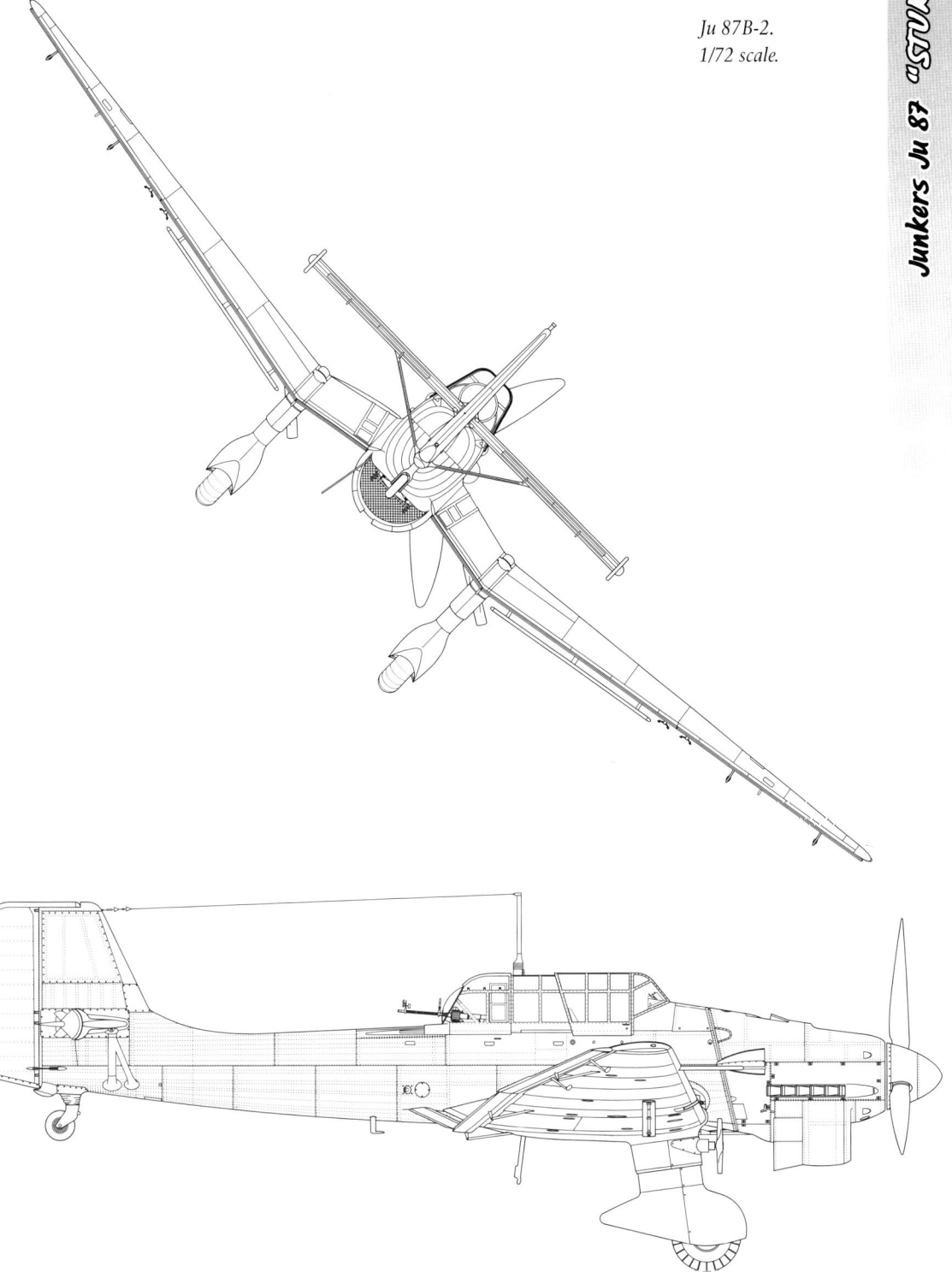

*Ju 87B-2.
1/72 scale.*

Junkers Ju 87 "STUKA"

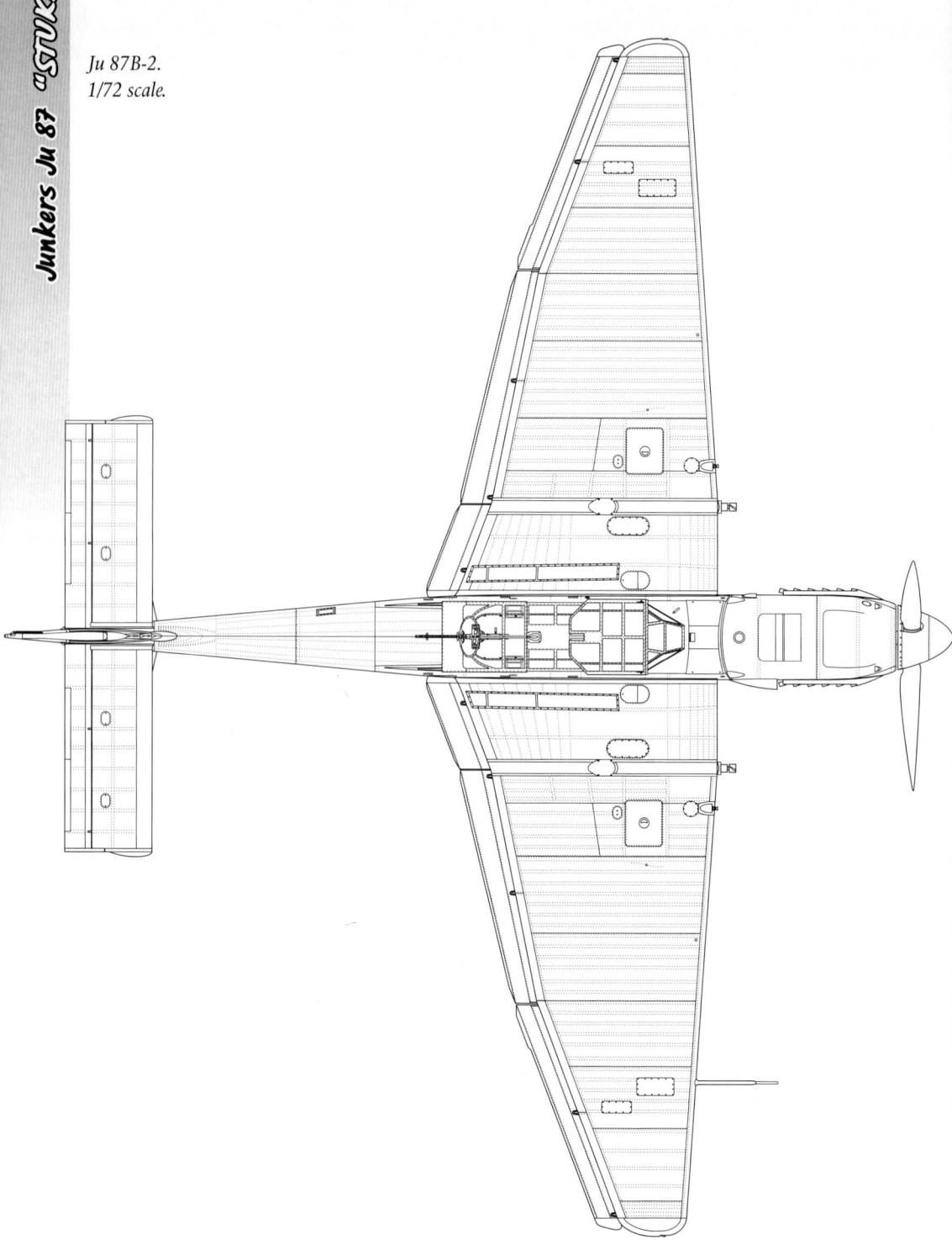

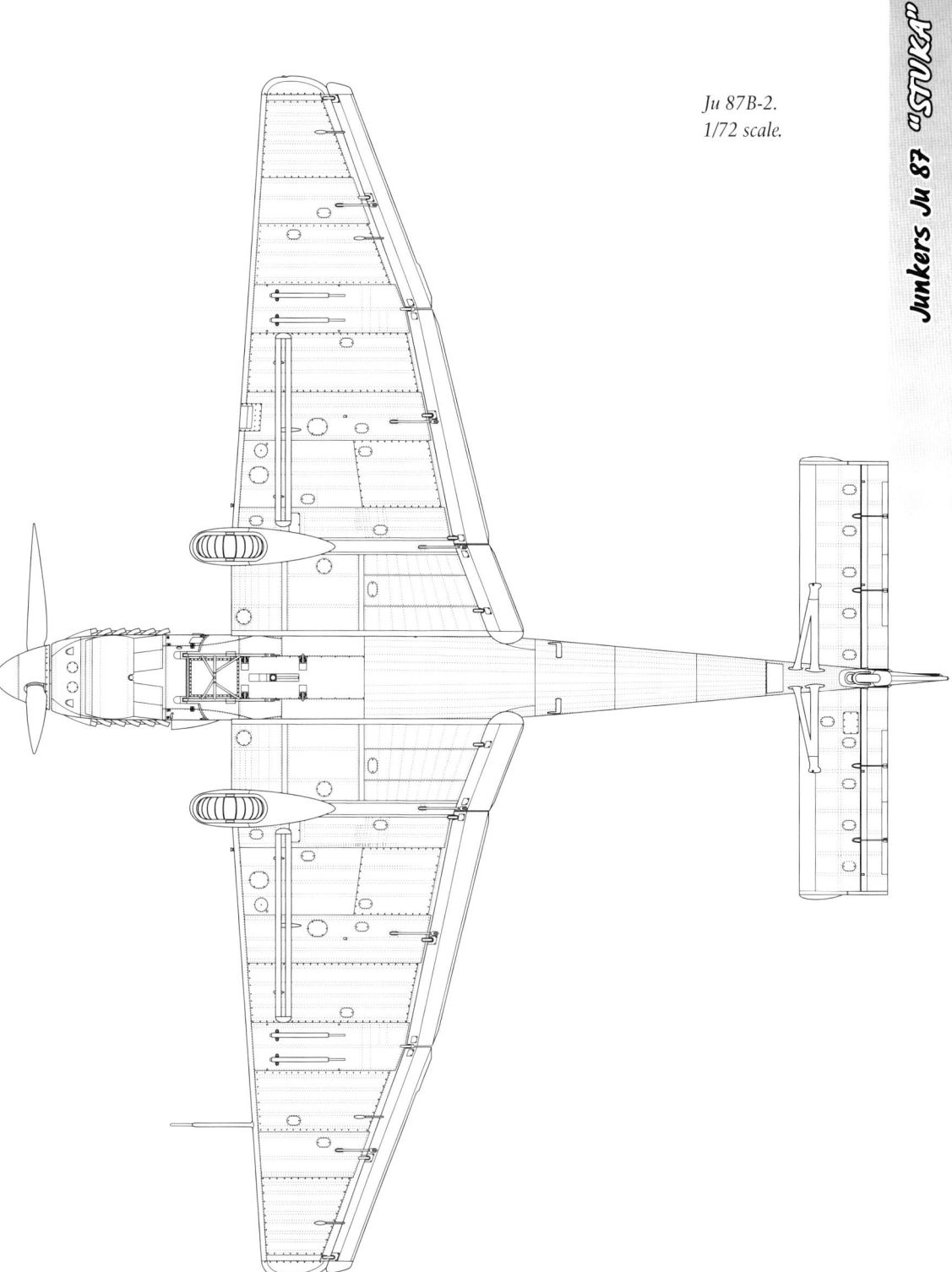

*Ju 87B-2.
1/72 scale.*

Junkers Ju 87 "STUKA"

33

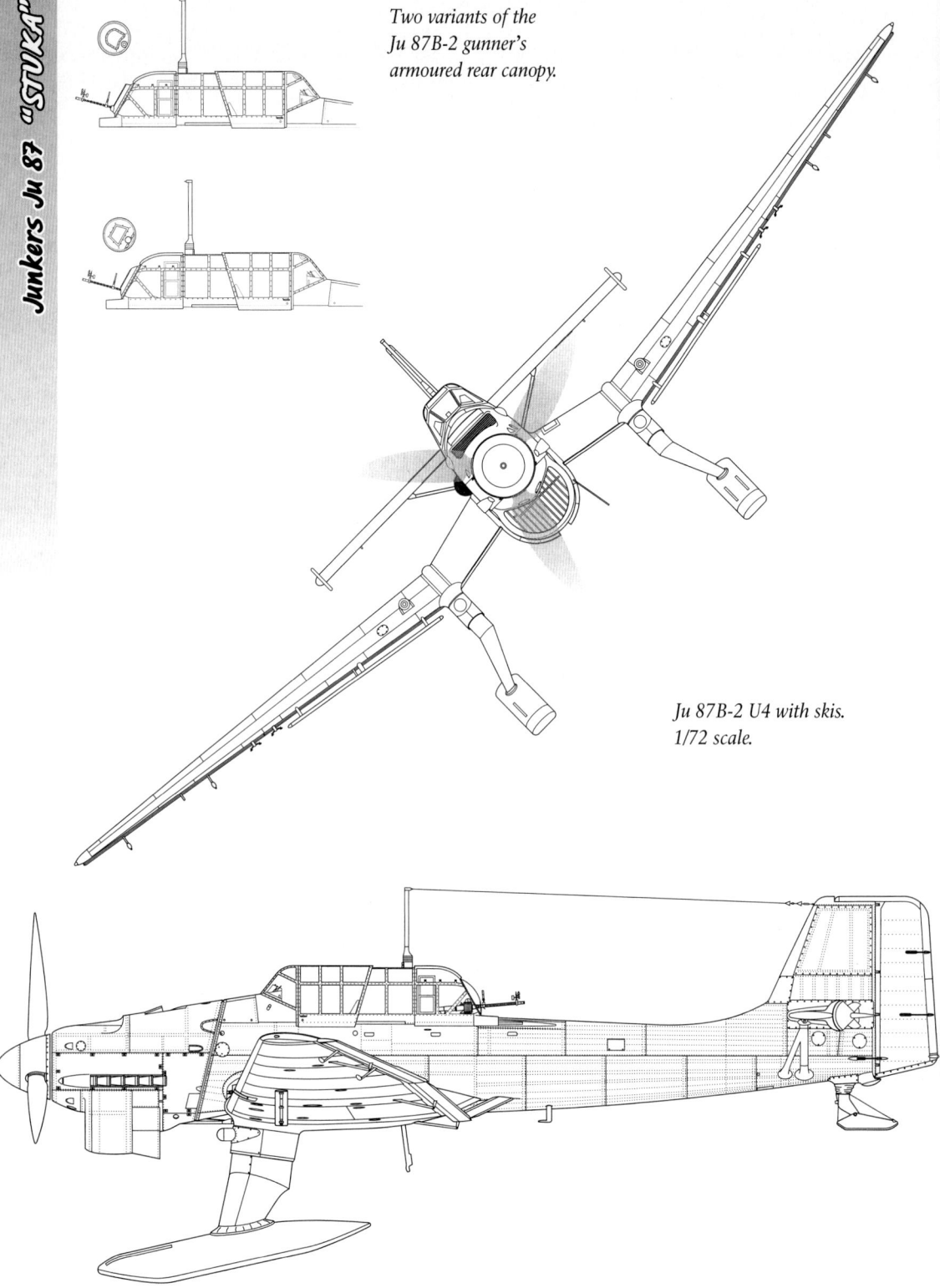

Two variants of the Ju 87B-2 gunner's armoured rear canopy.

Ju 87B-2 U4 with skis. 1/72 scale.

Junkers Ju 87 "STUKA"

Junkers Ju-87 R

A long-range version of the Ju-87 was developed during late 1939 and early 1940, with its designation reflecting the type's specialist nature rather than the linear sequence of development as in other models (*Reichweitenausfuhrung* - long range). The first prototype was built at Junkers' Dessau plant in late 1939, but manufacturing of the type was carried out exclusively by Weserflug at Bremen, between January and June 1940.

The Ju 87R was heavily based on the B model Stuka, and differed largely in terms of plumbing to allow a streamlined 300 litre fuel tank to be fitted to the bomb rack under each wing. The Ju 87R's oil system also differed from the B model. In all other respects, the B and R models were generally similar.

Production began with the R-1 which corresponded with the B-1. Only around 105 R-1s were built, as changes to the Ju 87B were introduced to the R model to create the Ju 87R-2. Initially, the long-range versions were converted from standard B models and indeed the R models were assigned Werk numbers in the same blocks that had been allocated to the B model production batches - W.Nr. 0500 upwards at Junkers and 5840 upwards at Weserflug. However, by the time of the introduction of the R-2, the long range variants were being built in their own right. The production of Ju 87R-2s continued from June 1940 to June 1941 and numbered 471 aircraft.

In fact, production of the long range Ju 87Extended beyond the expected end point of January 1941 and included 185 more aircraft than the 286 originally contracted for in Lieferplan 19. The Ju 87R-2 supplanted the ostensibly standard B model and for a time was the sole type in production, partly thanks

Ju 87R-2.

via R. Michulec.

Ju 87R-1 of 4./St.G 2, Greece 1941.
Stratus coll.

to development problems with the Ju 87D model but no doubt also thanks to the effectiveness of the Ju 87R, particularly in the anti-shipping role.

The R-3 version never left the drawing board, and doubts exist as to the exact nature of what this variant was proposed to be. Some sources claim it was intended as a glider tug[1] while others suggest an improved radio fit was the reason for the new designation. The R-4 on the other hand was intended

---

1 *The alleged use of the R-3 for glider towing is unlikely, as the modification allowing to tow gliders was not introduced until late spring/early summer 1942, and then on various Ju 87 versions.*

Details of the underwing fuel tank.
Stratus coll.

as a straightforward improvement of the R-2. It was suggested that the new long-range Stuka should adopt the more powerful Jumo 211J powerplant intended for the Ju 87D model, a lack of suitable engines meant that the R-4 as it appeared had only slight changes from the earlier model. The prototype, wearing the codes TJ+FP, flew around March 1941 and after tests at Rechlin, production started the following month - 145 of this type were built before production ceased in December 1941.

Exchanging the underwing fuel tanks, Ju 87R-1. Greece 1941.
Stratus coll.

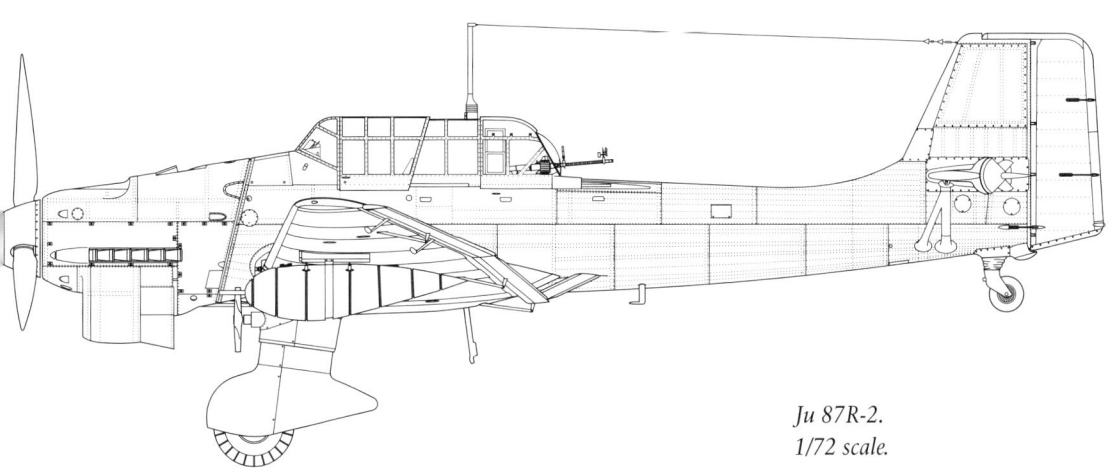

Ju 87R-2. 1/72 scale.

Tropical versions

A number of Stuka variants were developed from standard and long range Ju 87s for use in the North African and Mediterranean theatres. Examples of most Ju 87 variants were modified for hot climates throughout their careers, and these machines were commonly distinguished by the suffix 'trop'[1]. Alterations consisted chiefly of filters to prevent dust and sand affecting the radiator, carburettor, bomb racks and guns. Externally these aircraft only differed from their non-tropical equivalents in the larger and more angular carburettor intake.

In early 1941 tests with Junkers Ju 87 W.Nr. 5786 modified for hot climates were carried out at Rechlin by the Tropen Erprobungs Kommando (Tropics Testing Command). This aircraft was designated R-5, probably a Ju 87R-2 or R-4 suitably converted, and was possibly an attempt to produce a dedicated tropical Stuka. While 240 tropical versions were initially created by converting existing types at the Stuttgart-Sud plants (an operation that took 2-3 days), a dedicated Ju 87R trop was later put into production in April 1941 at Paderborn and Mönchengladbach. These began to be delivered to the *Luftwaffe* in May, and all but six of the 26 produced were tropical versions of the definitive R-4 long range Ju 87. Even with the modifications to protect the aircraft's vital systems from the ravages of sand and dust, the Jumo 211D's period for routine inspection was halved to 60 hours in tropical versions.

Ju 87R-2 trop of 4./St.G 2, Africa. Note the tropical filter.
Stratus coll.

---

1 RLM officials, irritated by the common application of the "trop" designator, issued a special letter on 17 December 1940 to remind that "tp" was the correct abbreviation. Nobody seemed to bother, though, and the "trop" suffix continued to be commonly used.

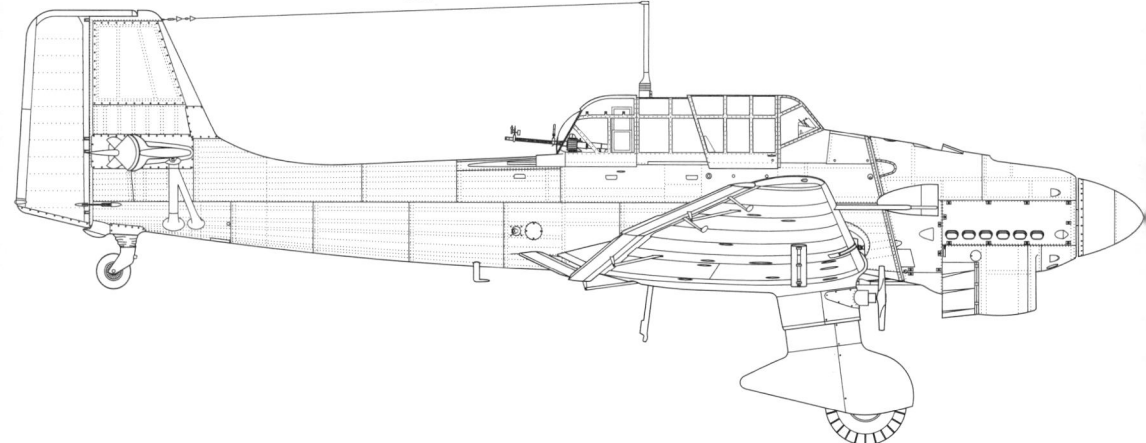

Junkers Ju 87C

From relatively early in the career of the Ju 87, a dedicated naval version was considered. This was to be based on the *Kriegsmarine's* proposed aircraft carriers, several of which were begun but never completed. The *Luftwaffe* had long been impressed by the development of naval dive bombing in the US and Japan, and the Stuka itself proved to be a formidable anti-shipping weapon in the Norwegian campaign of 1940 and later in the Mediterranean.

The *Luftwaffe* and *Kriegsmarine* fought over the control of naval and maritime aviation. In 1937 the matter was resolved when Hermann Göring's air force won control of what he dubbed "everything that flew in the Third Reich", and in August 1937 a *Luftwaffe* carrier-borne unit was therefore created. Simultaneously Göring initiated the construction and testing of naval prototypes. In fact, a mock-up of a naval Ju 87 had already existed since June, probably based on the Ju 87B. In September of that year Junkers officially commenced their naval dive bomber programme, with the designation Ju 87 Tr (for *Trägerflugzeug*, or carrier-borne aircraft).

Two prototypes were constructed from scratch, at the same time as the prototypes for the standard Ju 87B were being built, and these aircraft undertook trials until the end of 1937. The first of these was the V10, W.Nr. 4928, initially carrying the civil registration D-IHFH, but later wearing the military code TK+HD. The second was the V11, W.Nr. 4929, D-ILGM, later TV+OV. The first of these was an interim aircraft, and not fully navalised, but the V11 had folding wings and full naval equipment as tested on the mock-up. The aircraft shared many similarities with the Ju 87B but had a reinforced rear fuselage to compensate for the additional stresses imposed by the arrestor hook. The air-

Ju 87C-0, W.Nr. 0573, SH+DB, during a transfer flight to Italy. This aircraft was tested for use on **Aquila,** *an Italian carrier.*
via. R. Michulec.

craft also had catapult attachment points under the centre section for catapult launching.

The V10 appeared later than expected and did not fly until March 17th 1938, three months after the deadline that had originally been set by the RLM. The V11 took to the air for the first time on the 12th May. Both aircraft were sent for intensive tests at E-Stelle Travemünde. As a result of the delays in the prototype, a Ju 87A-1 had been modified with an arrestor hook and was used for testing before the genuine naval Stukas arrived.

The tests resulted in a number of modifications being required before the aircraft could enter service, including an improved wing folding mechanism which was installed in October at Dessau before the machine was returned to Travemünde. Ernst Udet himself was to take part in the hook-landing tests. The Ju 87 passed all of the preliminary stages, the RLM agreed to a pre-production run of ten naval Stukas, designated Ju 87C. The Weserflug factory was commissioned to build these aircraft between April and July 1940. The pre-production machines were to be followed by a full production run of 120 aircraft. The carrier-use trials continued, with the emphasis on catapult launching. After a month-long programme with the Ju 87 V10 on the FL 24 catapult at Kiel shipyards, the Ju 87 was cleared for carrier use.

In the spring on 1940, the first Ju 87Cs began construction at the Weserflug plant, but there was some disagreement over the pre-production batch and eventually the number of these required was halved to five. In fact, series production began right away and the first five aircraft from the line were earmarked for trials, designated Ju 87C-1. The first two aircraft W.Nr. 0570 and 0571 were completed in March 1941. The next two, 0569 (with the military code GD+FB) and 0572 (GD+FC) were delivered in April, and 0573 (SH+DB) was completed in June.

Apart from naval modifications, the Ju 87Cs closely resembled the long range R-2 model, with plumbing in the wings for external fuel tanks, Jumo 211D engines and broad-bladed VS 11 propellers. The Ju 87C's wings were slightly shorter than the standard, having been clipped to 13 m (42 ft 3 in) to facilitate folding. Wing folding was electrically operated and arranged so the wings swung backwards to lie against the fuselage. With wings folded, width was reduced to 5 m (16 ft 3 in). The under wing racks for 50 kg bombs were retained.

All five machines were sent for tests at Travemünde and the Junkers airframe and engine factories. These trials took place until the end of 1941, although during this time official interest in the programme waned. The number of available Ju 87C-1s undergoing the tests gradually reduced as failures occurred and there were delays in the delivery of replacement components such as propellers. One aircraft (W.Nr. 0572) was cannibalised for spares to keep others airworthy. In the spring of 1942, another round of hook landing tests commenced, but by this stage, only Stuka VD+LA was available to carry them out. By 1943, only the Ju 87C-1 W.Nr. 0573 was used extensively, when it underwent a special tour of trials in Italy with a view to equipping the Italian aircraft carrier *Aquila*, then under construction, with Ju 87s. Later, three other aircraft (0571, 0572, and the Ju 87 V10) were sent to the same country for field trials with Fliegerkorps XI. Tests of the model continued, but were increasingly sporadic. Eventually, with the cancellation of the aircraft carrier *Graf Zeppelin*, there was no need for the Ju 87C and the special carrier unit was disbanded. Some of the Ju 87Cs did see action in the 1939 Polish campaign, operating from land bases, but those that survived were eventually converted back to B status.

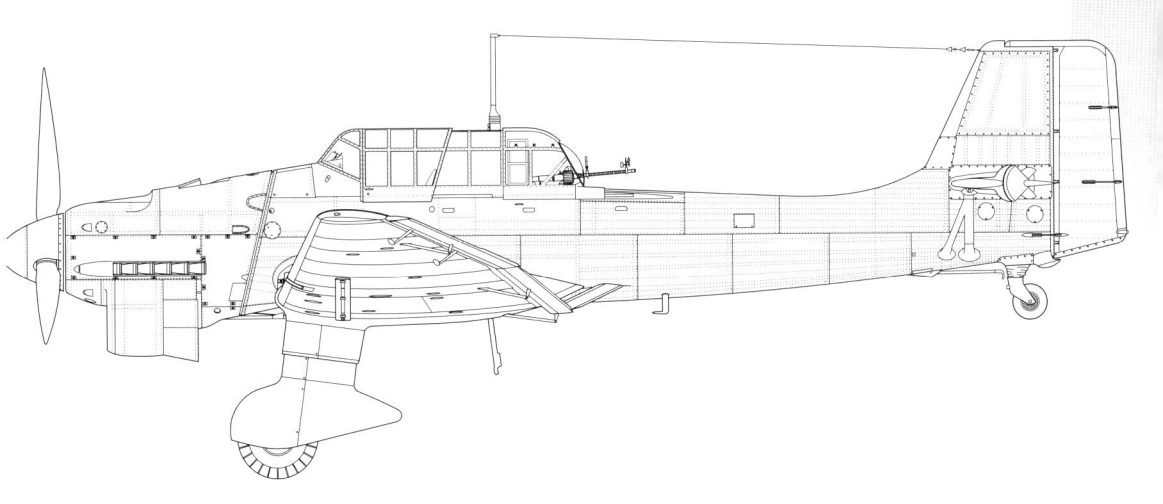

Ju 87C-0.
1/72 scale.

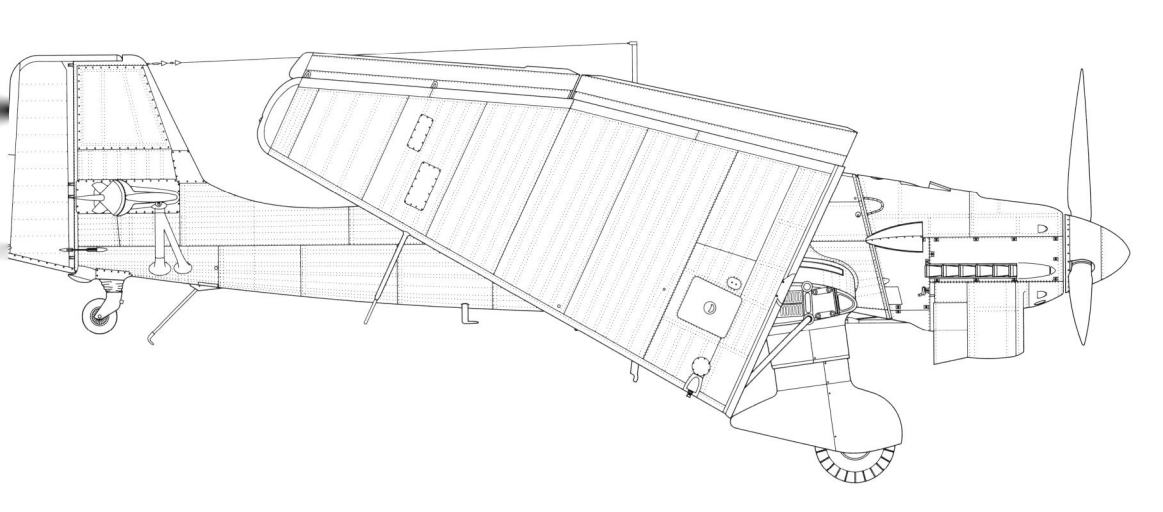

Junkers Ju 87D

As with the B-model, the next standard version of the Ju 87 was planned to be a major improvement over existing versions. This was the Ju 87D which like the B had numerous external changes to distinguish it from its predecessors.

The most significant change planned was again the installation of a more powerful engine to increase both performance and weapon carrying ability. The Jumo 211F, J and K types offered 1,350-1,450 PS (1,330-1,430 hp) but were also larger and heavier than the 211D. The new powerplant was 404 mm (15.5in) longer, and had an entirely new cooling system and radiators. This once again necessitated substantial reprofiling of the nose, and the opportunity was taken to improve the aircraft's aerodynamics in this area. Junkers also designed a more aerodynamically efficient canopy.

The new engine offered significantly greater load carrying potential – over 1,700 kg of bombs could now be delivered, although this required compromises in other areas.

Unfortunately, the new powerplant suffered numerous problems with its development and the final decision to fit the developed Stuka with the updated 211 was not made until the autumn of 1940. In October a Jumo 211J was fitted to Ju 87B-1 (W.Nr. 0321, with the civil registration D-IGDK) but trials of this installation were blighted by repeated engine failures. Another Ju 87B (W.Nr. 2291) was used as an aerodynamic prototype of the new dive bomber with mocked-up canopy, while the true Ju 87D prototype, the Junkers V-21 (W.Nr. 0536, civil registration D-INRF), appeared in November 1940. This machine was used for manufacturer tests, although it seems that for the first nine months of its career it was fitted with the older Jumo 211D engine. The second and third prototypes designated V22 and V23 (W.Nr. 0540, coded SF+TY and W.Nr. 0542, coded PB+UB) initially also flew with the older powerplant.

The prototypes were used for intensive testing, with the first continuing manufacturer trials and the second going to Rechlin for official RLM tests.

Ju 87 V22, one of the Ju 87D prototypes, with 1000 kg bomb.
via R. Michulec.

Later the third prototype joined the first for testing by Junkers. Between April and August 1941 the three prototypes were finally fitted with the Jumo 211J powerplants intended for production versions. The V22 was fitted with a Jumo 211J in April 1941 before being sent to Rechlin to assess its suitability for service acceptance the following month. The third prototype, the V23, received a Jumo 211J that month and was used by the manufacturer to assess flying characteristics, equipment and the engine. The first prototype, the V21, was finally fitted with a Jumo 211F in August 1941 and used to test the engine, cooling system and armament.

Two more prototypes were completed in March 1941 and flown around July. They joined the test programme in the autumn with V24 (W.Nr. 0544, coded BK+EE) further contributing to the development of the D-1 version during which it was slightly damaged. Meanwhile the V25 (W.Nr. 0530, coded BK+EF) formed the basis for the tropical sub-variant.

In the late summer to early autumn of 1941 the problems with the Jumo 211J engines had largely been solved and they became available in sufficient numbers to put the Ju 87D into full production. Therefore in September 1941, the first two Ju 87D-1s left the factory - three months later than had been originally intended under *Lieferplan 19/2*. Bad weather delayed the delivery of Ju 87D-1s to the *Luftwaffe* until December but even then only 61 aircraft had been completed. Of these, eight were retained by E-Stelle Rechlin for service trials, but these machines later followed the rest of the first production D-1s to frontline units. The first action seen by the Ju 87D was at Leningrad in January 1942. There were 592 D-1s built, with serials of W.Nr. 2000 upwards, up to approximately 2600.

An improved Ju 87D, the D-3, first appeared in May 1942, with serials from W.Nr. 2600 upwards, although from early 1943 the RLM changed to a five-digit system with D-3s in production starting from 31100 upwards to 31600. In early 1943 the system was altered again, and six-digit W.Nr. serials were introduced. D-3s then in production received number blocks of 100001 upwards and 110300 upwards.

Ju 87 V21, SF+TY, one of the Ju 87D prototypes.
via R. Michulec.

The new aircraft differed little from the D-1 and most of the changes were internal, structural or to facilitate simpler production. There had been 1,559 D-3s assembled by the autumn of 1943. Of these, 599 were made by Weserflug at Bremen, and 960 at Weserflug's new plant at Tempelhof. Junkers also built a new plant, at Berlin, which began working in early 1941 and all Junkers-built Ju 87Ds were produced here.

A number of modifications were made to the D-1 and D-3 during the period they were in production. These ranged from the relatively minor, such as fitting additional data plates listing the aircraft type and serial number, to relatively major changes to the airframe structure. Fuel and oil pipes were replaced with wider examples to allow a better flow of fluids to vital systems. A ski undercarriage was developed[1] in January 1942, which was later replaced by a dedicated modification kit (see below).

As well as improving of the performance of the Stuka, the D model also saw numerous improvements to its armament. The cockpit was once again revised and a new gunsight, the Revi C/12D, was introduced. Another significant development was the inclusion of two 150 l fuel tanks, one in each wing. The Ju 87D received a further developed radio with the FuG 25 set and Peil GIV RDF unit, which was moved further up in the fuselage to a location just behind the rear cockpit.

The variety of under-wing stores that could be carried increased significantly on the D model. Each wing had three different mounting points on which could be fitted two ETC 50 bomb racks or one ETC 500 bomb rack – the former allowed two 50kg (110 lb) bombs to be carried under each wing, while

Ju 87D-1 Rüstsatz B, probably W.Nr. 2070, GD+VH, during trials with additional armour, winter 1941/42.

via R. Michulec.

---

1   *The dates are approximate; they indicate the period in the year rather than an exact date. The process of development (JFM), testing (E-Stelle) and acceptance (RLM) of a modification lasted for 1-5 months. The modification was introduced in production after RLM acceptance, or even during the process.*

the latter allowed a single 250-500kg (550-1,100 lb) bomb under each wing. These could be covered by a fairing when not in use to reduce drag. Alternatively the ETC 500 hard points could be adapted to carry a pylon-mounted 200 litre (44 Imp gal) fuel tank. The undercarriage was improved yet again to deal with the ever increasing all-up weight, with the addition of larger, 840mm x 300mm, tyres. Problems were experienced with the D-1's undercarriage which were solved by replacing the D-1 main and tail units with those of the older B-2 model, though later the Ju 87D undercarriage was corrected and production could continue with the original system. Later still, in March 1943, the main undercarriage was modernised again, by replacing the fork with a new unit, which was mounted 90mm (3.5 in) further aft, and increasing the length of the leg by 12 mm (1/2 in). The modification appeared towards the end of D-3 production, and was standard in the D-5 model. From April 1943, all Ju 87-Ds were modified with the addition of explosive cartridges that allowed the undercarriage to be jettisoned.

The new Stuka was a much more versatile and capable machine than its predecessors. It could deliver large bombs that could only be carried previously by medium bombers such as the He 111 and Ju 88, although to lift the heaviest bomb loads, fuel had to be reduced and the wing guns' ammunition removed. It could also be fitted with ski undercarriage, used as a glider tug, fitted with long range fuel tanks, and even used as a torpedo bomber. The armament that could be fitted to any particular Ju 87D was characterised by a complex alphanumeric system known as *Rüstsatze* (Conversion Kit). Thus, M1 denoted the main rack under the fuselage, able to carry 250-1000 kg bombs, M2 - two under-wing racks for 250 kg bombs, M3 - racks positioned in the same place but for 50-70 kg bombs.

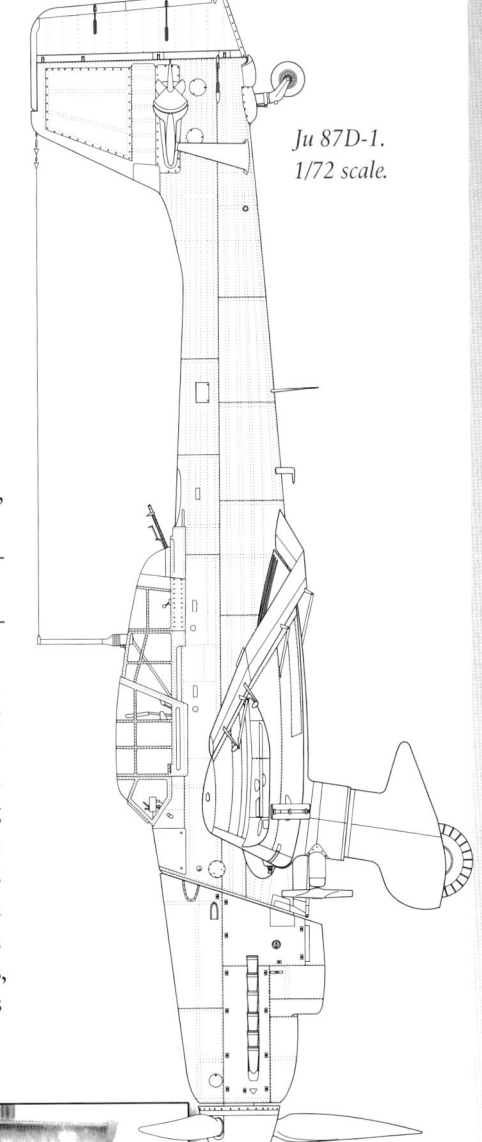

Ju 87D-1. 1/72 scale.

Ju 87D-1, W.Nr. 2302, just after completation, spring 1942.
via. R. Michulec.

The carriage of drop tanks was designated *Rüstsatz B*, glider towing fit was *Rüstsatz S*. This was introduced in April 1942, but was unsatisfactory and required two further modifications in August of that year before it was effective. The addition of flame dampers was known as *Rüstsatz FLA*. Other equipment which could be fitted included gun cameras, and winter or desert survival kits. In addition three overall equipment fits were designated *Rüstzustand* (modified version) *A* (dive bomber), *B* (torpedo bomber) and *C* (ski undercarriage).

In addition to the above, heavier ordnance could be carried; such as the PC 1700 (1,704 kg, 3,749 lb) armour piercing bomb which for the first time meant that the Ju 87Could inflict terminal damage to capital ships with a single bomb. The Ju 87D could also carry SC 1700 (1,704 kg, 3,749 lb) and SC 1800 (1,835 kg, 4,037 lb) bombs, the latter colloquially known as 'Satan', which were devastatingly effective against enemy fortifications. These heavier bombs were in reality only carried by the small number of Stukas which had the ETC 2000/XII bomb rack. Only experienced Ju 87 pilots could hope to take off successfully with a load of this weight, and a good runway was essential. To add to these complications, the heavier bombs suffered from faulty fuses which meant that they often failed to detonate. Until this was resolved Ju 87Ds did not carry these weapons.

The most common way the Ju 87D's load-lifting capabilities were exploited was to load it with three bombs up to 500 kg (1,100 kg) and a full load of fuel and ammunition, which still did not exceed the maximum take-off weight of 6,600 kg (14,520 lb).

Modifications continued throughout the production run. In February 1942 revised, and more reliable, attachments for the nose cowling panels were introduced. In March 1942, a support was added to the rear MG 81Z to prevent the gunner from shooting the tail of his own aircraft with its own machine gun fire, and a catch was also fitted to the rear cockpit guns to secure them during violent manoeuvring.

Modifications to strengthen the wing and radiator installation were introduced to Stuka production lines in April 1942. This involved mounting struts that connected the wing spar to the armour plate installed to protect the underside of the radiators, two struts at the front and two at the rear. Further changes to the aircraft's armour were brought in from May 1943, which included armour plate under the cockpit, reflecting the increasing change in the Stuka's role from dive bomber to ground attack aircraft. Armoured windscreen glass had been added since June 1942.

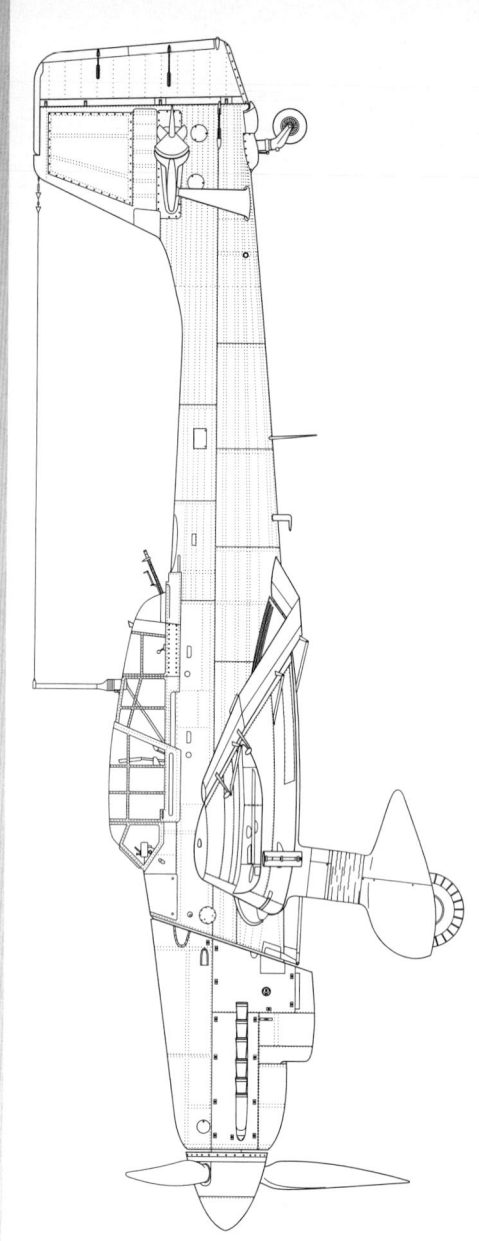

Ju 87D-3, early.
1/72 scale.

*Ju 87D-3 (late).
1/72 scale.*

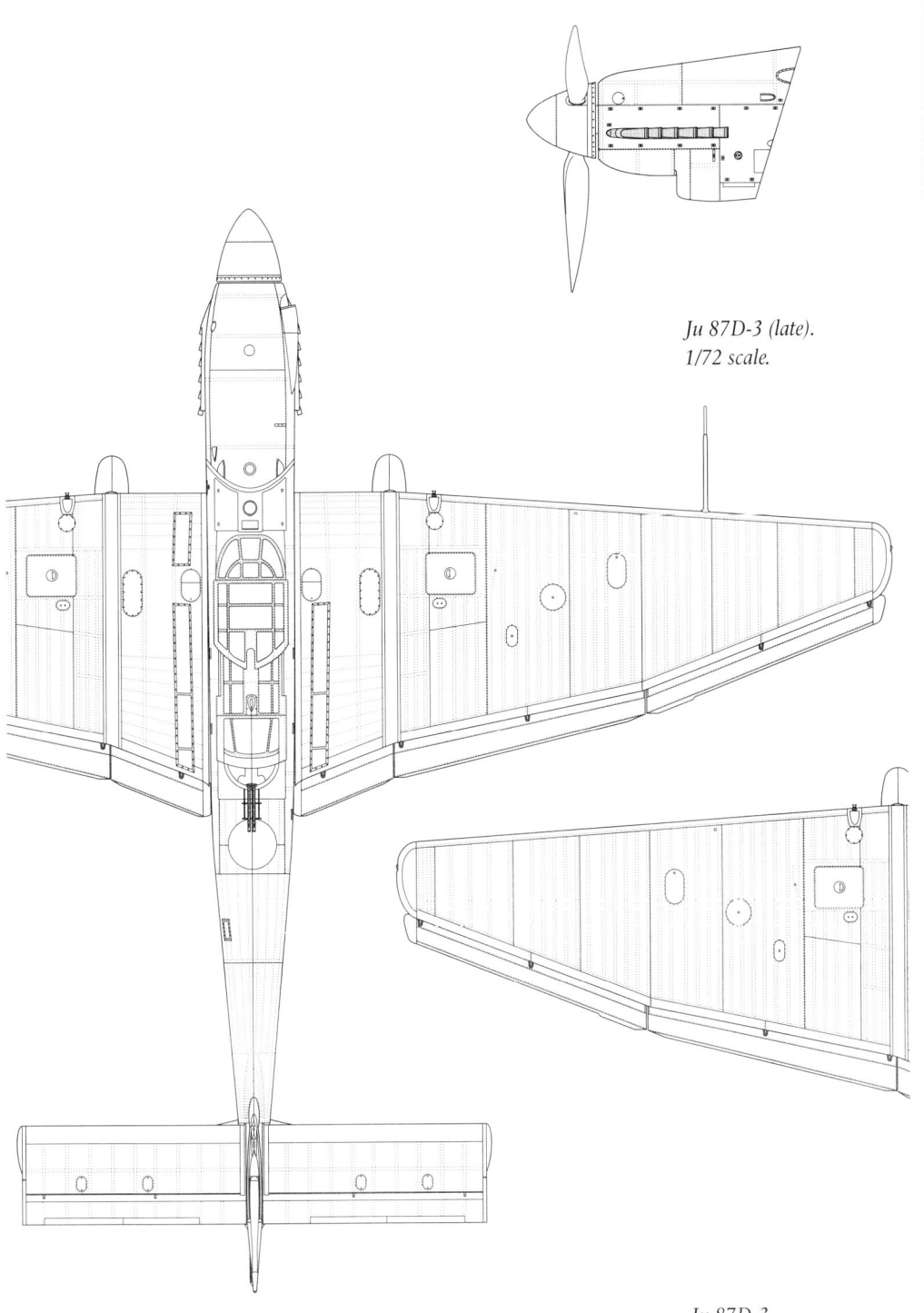

*Ju 87D-3.
1/72 scale.*

Junkers Ju 87 "STUKA"

47

Ju 87D-1 of St.G 3, North Africa, spring 1943.
via R. Michulec.

The changing role was also reflected in a further development programme which commenced in the autumn of 1942 to increase the number of small calibre machine guns. This was intended to allow Stuka crews to attack enemy infantry more effectively. These consisted of the special WB 81 containers which could be fitted to the under wing and fuselage bomb racks. They enabled two forward-firing gun pods to be added which could be fired by the pilot in addition to the existing wing guns, while a rear-facing pod in the central under-fuselage position could be operated by the gunner - although this latter weapon was later deleted. The modification was used on the Eastern front although it is not believed to have been widely adopted.

In August 1942 modifications of the fuel injection system were introduced. Also that month improvements were made to the pitot tube inside the wing. At the same time, a widespread programme of reinforcement for fuselage frames 7-12 was carried out across the entire Ju 87 Fleet including all those in service as well incorporating the changes on the production line. The following month the engine cowling was altered to include a duct to direct hot air to the power plant. In December 1942 the main bomb racks were modified to carry the SD 500 bomb, and MG 81Z ammunition belt containers were improved.

A highly specialised development of the D-3 was proposed and designated the Ju 87D-3Ag (Ag for Agentenflugzeug). This was intended for insertion of espionage agents in special nacelles over the wings. This was not pursued, perhaps fortunately for the agents in question.

The D-4 was intended to be a specialised torpedo bomber prototype, rather than as the previous other versions, a dive bomber with supplementary torpedo carrying ability. The prototype, designated V25 by Junkers, was modified from the prototype for the tropical D-1, W.Nr. 0530, which was coded BK+EF, and had first flown in July 1941. In November of that year, the aircraft's modification into a torpedo bomber was completed and was included in the trials of

Details of Ju 87D-3 canopy.

Stratus coll.

the Ju 87Cs at Travemünde in December. An earlier prototype, the V19 (W.Nr. 4930, VN+EN), had flown as early as February 1940 and was allocated for early trials of torpedo carrying capability. The results of these tests were favourable, but volume production of the Ju 87D-3 type was beginning so there was no capacity to continue with a torpedo carrying version of the D-1. Instead, plans were made for Ju 87D-4 that would be a dedicated torpedo version, equivalent to the dive bombing D-5. Two aircraft, including W.Nr. 2292, were taken from the D-3 production line that had been completed in mid April and earmarked as prototypes for the D-4.

The RLM requested 10 D-4s for trials, but it was increasingly clear that improved anti-aircraft armament and increased air cover for convoys meant that torpedo aircraft needed considerably greater performance than the Ju 87 offered to avoid unacceptable losses. The Junkers Ju 88 and Heinkel He

One of the first Ju 87D-5s at a factory airfield, autumn 1943.

via R. Michulec.

111 developed for torpedo carriage proved much more suitable due to their better performance and greater range, so the Ju 87D-4 was dropped after one or two prototypes were built.

In the Spring of 1943 another improved version of the standard Ju 87D was introduced to supercede the D-3. The D-5 first appeared in prototype form in June 1943 as the V30 and entered production as early as July 1943. However, the modifications that would lead to the D-5 went back to the summer of 1941 when fitting the MG 151/20 cannon in place of the normal wing mounted armament was first mooted.

The Ju 87D-5 had a redesigned wing, with a modified root to allow the fitting of the cannon and magazines of 250 rounds, and a new tip that increased the overall area to reduce wing-loading. The wingspan of the D-5 was 15 m (48 ft 9 in) as opposed to 13.8 m (44 ft 10 in) in the earlier models, and the wing area was increased from 31.90 m² to 32.60 m².

Ju 87D over Russia, 1943. Stratus coll.

Other improvements included the Revi 16D gun sight and new FuG 16Z (later FuG 16ZS) radio in later D-5 batches. The Peilrufanlage RDF equipment was also fitted to the later D-5s from summer 1944.

The D-5's bomb load was also increased over previous D models with the introduction of new under wing racks that could accept 70 kg (154 lb) bombs instead of the 50 kg (110 lb) bombs that the earlier D models could carry. Another indicator of the Stuka's changing role was the addition of the BZA-2 sight which could be used for level-bombing at low altitudes.

Few changes were introduced during production of the D-5 model, and those were relatively minor. Slight alterations were made to the armour on the underside of the engine, the cannon's ammunition feed was improved and a redesigned fuel system for the fuselage tank was imposed from aircraft W.Nr. 130971 upwards. Production of this model lasted for around a year, during which 1,178 were built (771 of them at Bremen). The machines had serials in small blocks within the range of W.Nr. 130500 to 142900.

A propaganda photo of Staffeln commander Dr. Maximilian Otte and his pilots after his 700th combat sortie. Stratus coll.

Although the role of the Ju 87 was changing, and many alterations had been made to the design to reflect that, it was still considered to be chiefly a dive bomber, and up to this point retained the equipment needed for this operation - airbrakes and bomb crutch. However, the fortunes of the pure dive bomber were waning and *Luftwaffe* high command and the RLM increasingly wished to replace Ju 87s with Focke-Wulf Fw 190 fighter-bombers. This was made more obvious by the lack of a requirement for a direct successor to the Ju 87. The Allies were steadily increasing their air superiority on all fronts that pushed the *Luftwaffe* onto a defence footing and eroded the Ju 87's traditional mission which was to support an advancing army while benefiting from a state of air superiority.

This also had an impact on the tactics used by Ju 87 squadrons. The situation on the front line no longer left much scope for the Stuka's traditional tactic - the devastating attack by an entire squadron on a concentrated target. This took too much time and left the dive bombers too vulnerable to interception by fighters, and with too few fighters to provide enough support, losses would have been unacceptable.

Therefore, Stukas began to operate in smaller groups operating independently in 'hit and run' attacks on smaller targets such as columns of infantry or motorised forces, and troops in action. Despite the enormous success of the dive bomber earlier in the war, combat was now ironically turning towards Wolfram von Richthofen's favoured ground attack fighter-bomber style of warfare. Indeed, by the end of the war, only one *Luftwaffe* Gruppe was equipped with the Ju 87D - the III./SG 2 had 34 D-5s on the 12th April 1945.[2] (plus a further 21 of the tank busting G model.)

---

2   Officially all Gustavs were in the 10.(Pz)/SG 2, but photos prove beyond doubt that no less than 2-3 Ju 87Gs were in the Stab/SG 2.

Ju 87D in winter camouflage, Russia.

via. R. Michulec.

Junkers Ju 87 "STUKA"

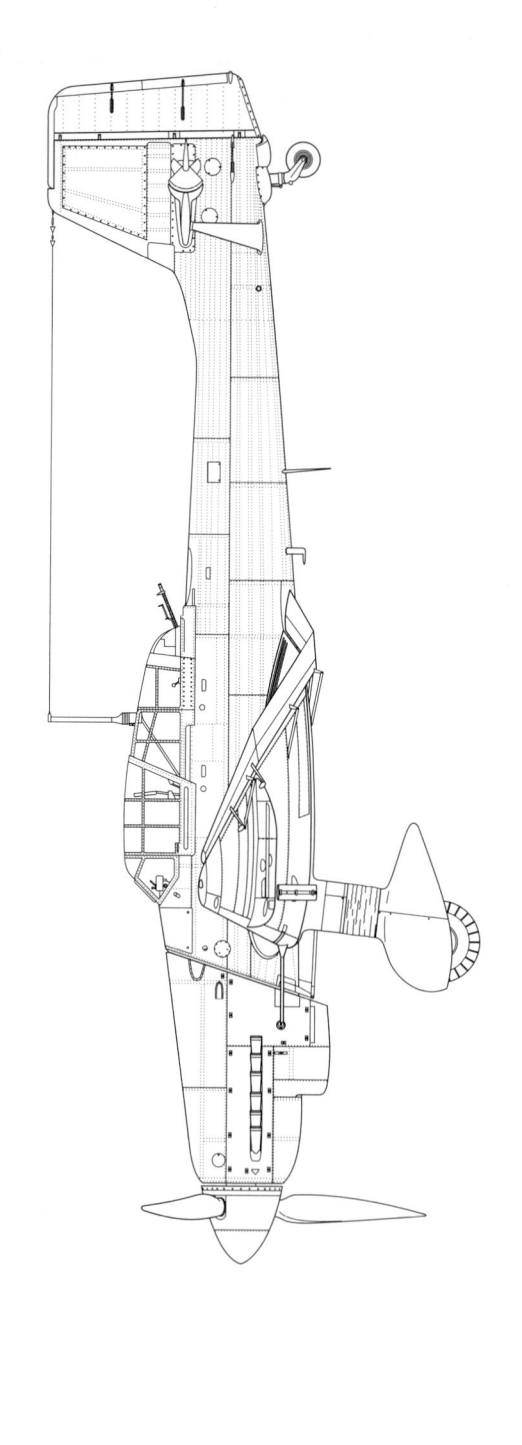

Ju 87D-5.
1/72 scale.

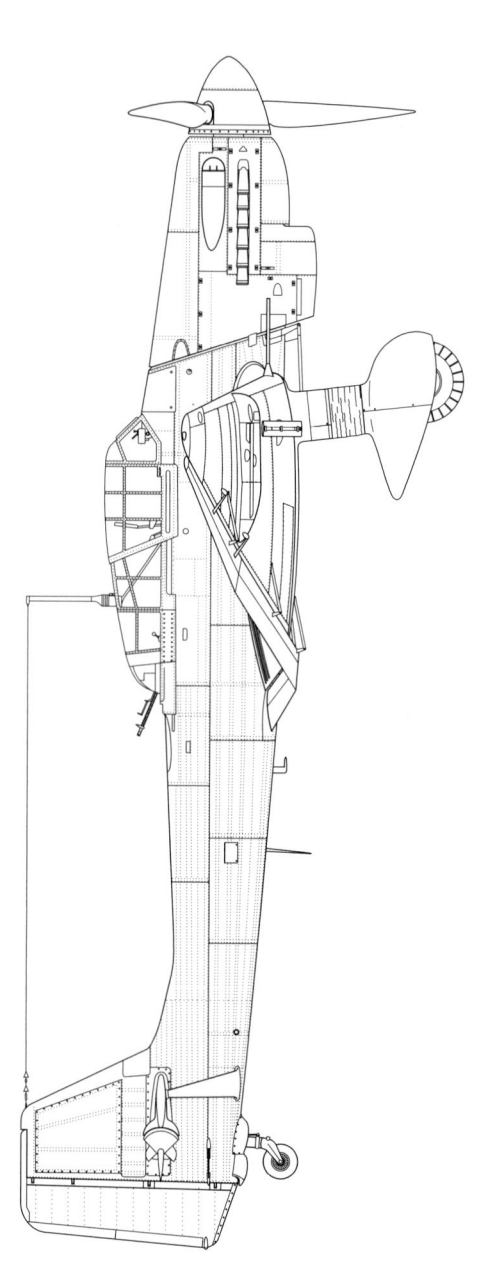

Junkers Ju 87 "STUKA"

*Ju 87D-5.
1/72 scale.*

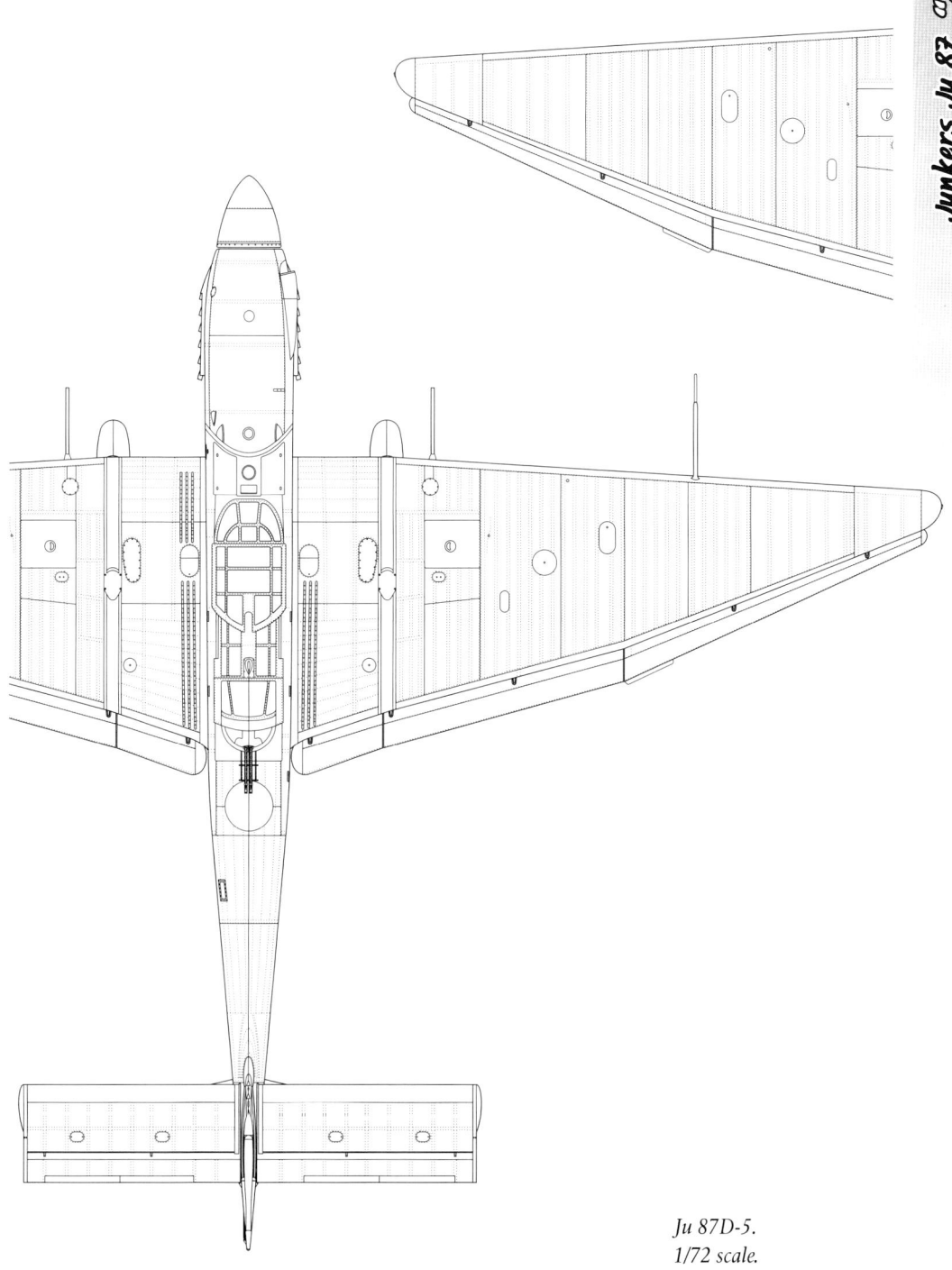

Junkers Ju 87 "STUKA"

Ju 87D-5.
1/72 scale.

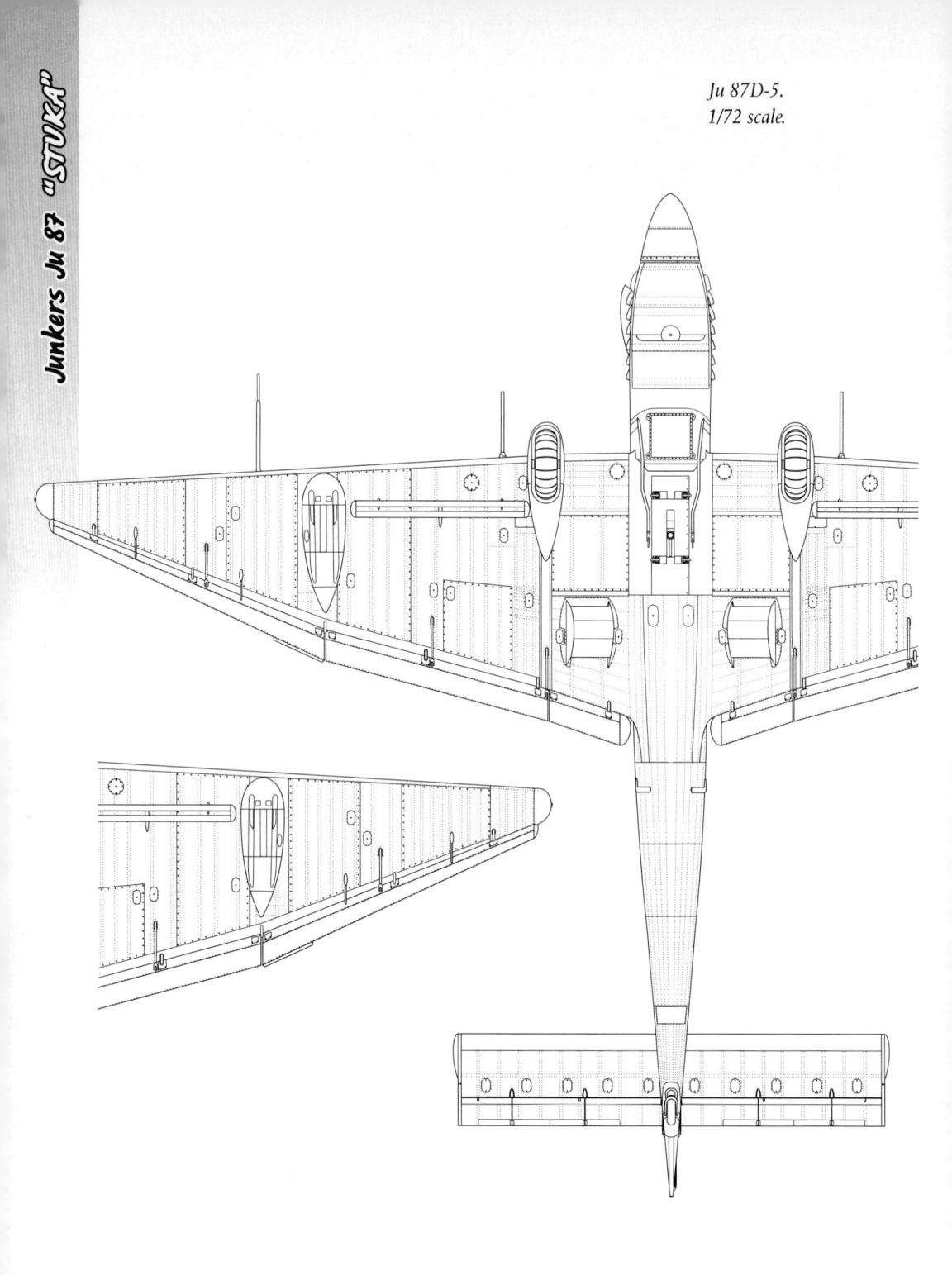

Ju 87D-1 over Russia.
D. Bernád coll.

Right: Ju 87D taxying after a mission.
D. Bernád coll.

Ju 87D-5s in winter camouflage over Russia.
D. Bernád coll.

Ju 87D after forced landing.

D. Bernád coll.

*Below:
Two photos of Ju 87D flown by Oblt. Ritter. Photos were taken on 21.04.1943 at Novorossijsk, Russia.*

D. Bernád coll.

Junkers Ju 87D night versions

Specialised night versions of the Ju 87 Appeared in 1944. Some sources claim the night Stukas appeared in the autumn of 1943. However, it seems more likely that variants fully converted for use at night did not appear until the following year. It appears that two derivatives of the Junkers Ju 87D line may have been developed into specific night attack aircraft, although some uncertainty exists over the exact nature of these types. Possible uses include harassment attacks on enemy positions or even as night fighters to stave off night raids by Soviet Po-2 biplanes.

Flame dampers for the Ju 87's exhaust first appeared in September 1942 and it was proposed to fit these to all models still in service, namely the B and R models as well as the D variants as these allowed night flying without visual detection. In August 1944 a modification programme was developed by Junkers for night-specific versions of the Stuka. This included a number of minor changes including fitting an artificial horizon on the main instrument panel, replacing the standard sight with a Revi C/12N, or Revi 16D/N night sight, special cockpit lighting to allow instruments to be read without affecting the pilot's night vision, an extra navigation light under the nose and blast tubes on wing cannon and machine guns. Photographs that purport to show night versions suggest that not all these proposed modifications were always fitted - for example, gun blast tubes are often absent. It has been suggested that the night versions of the Ju 87D were designated Ju 87D-7 and D-8, although other documents suggest that these designations were assigned to early model Ju 87Ds that had been updated with the Ju 87D-5 wing. Alternatively, D-3s and

Ju 87D-5/N (D-8) in spring 1944.

via R. Michulec.

*Ju 87D-7.
1/72 scale.*

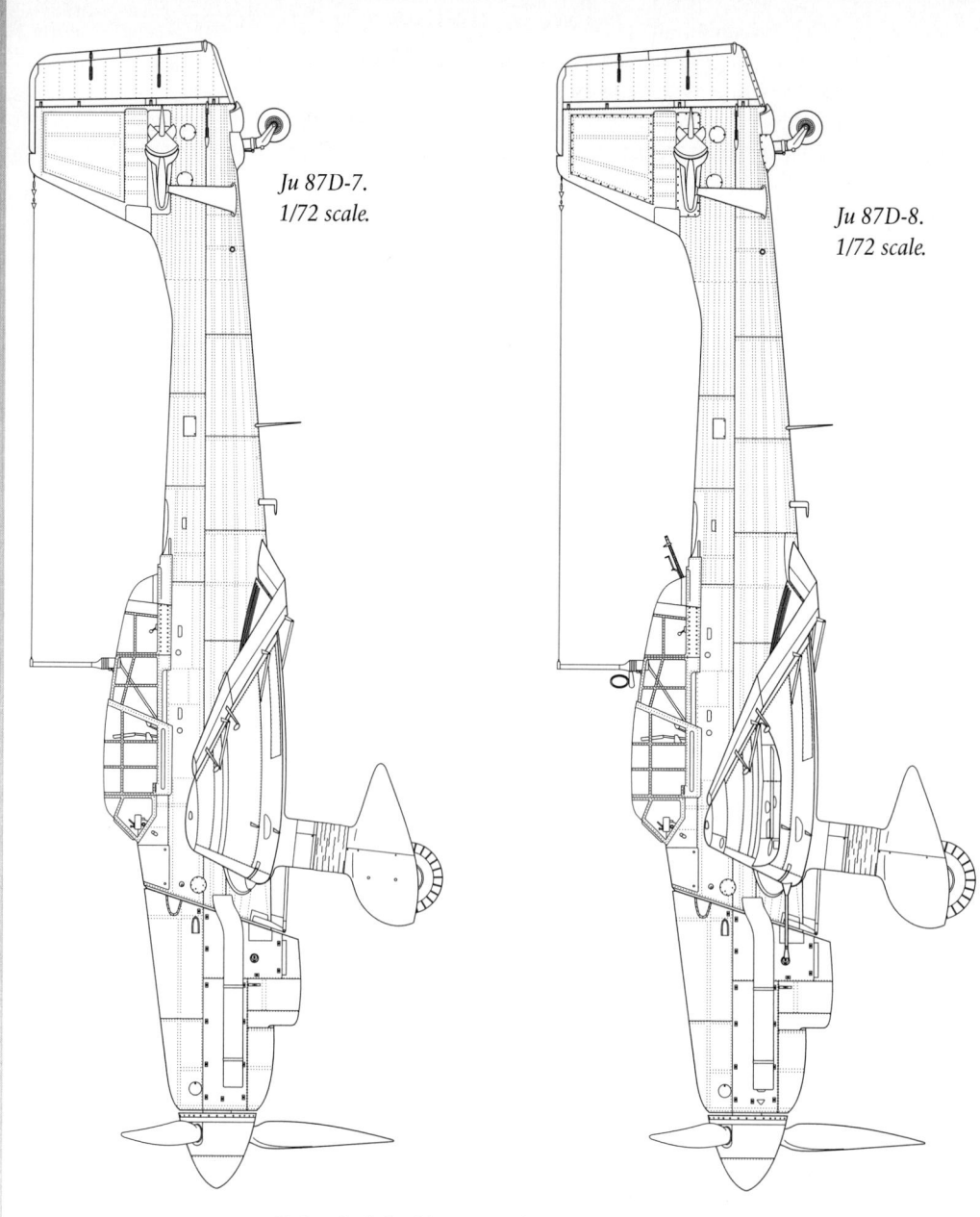

*Ju 87D-8.
1/72 scale.*

D-5s which had been retrofitted with the night modifications were known as D-3/N and D-5/N (N for Nacht).

In fact, special night squadrons known as Nachtschlachtgruppen (NSGrn) were set up as early as March 1942 and some Ju 87Ds were delivered to these units to replace the obsolete biplanes they had previously been equipped with. These appear to be earlier model Ju 87Ds with wing MG 17 machine guns still fitted. However, the modification programme was a rolling one with developments added to aircraft in service as they became available. Air brakes were often removed and some aircraft were fitted with the FuG 101 radio altimeter for more accurate assessment of height at night. Later D-5/N Stukas were apparently fitted with more powerful Jumo 211P engines of 1,500 PS (1,480 hp), though this was also true of non-night flying Stukas.

The delivery of night flying Stukas continued even after production of the type had ended, suggesting that the modified aircraft were drawn from stocks of reserve aircraft held by *Luftwaffe* HQ. Four Gruppen operated night flying Stukas in 1944, rising to six by the war's end, although all but one used other types as well.

Junkers Ju 87E

The E model Stuka was a second attempt to create an aircraft carrier-based Ju 87, this time based on the D model dive bomber. Unlike the earlier Ju 87C, the proposed Ju 87E was to be a torpedo bomber as well as a dive bomber, using the experience of the torpedo carrying land-based D-1/B and D-5/B.

The Ju 87C prototypes were re-employed on this programme in the summer of 1942, while three Ju 87Ds (VD+LB, VD+LA and SF+TW) were sent to E-Stelle Travemünde, and were used for trial catapult take-offs and radio tests. In October 1942 plans were made to prepare 10 prototype and pre-production Ju 87Es, with the first to be ready in November 1942 followed a year later by the production machines. However, once again work on the carrier-based Ju 87 was cancelled, due to the changing military doctrines in the Third Reich. When Admiral Dönitz took over from Admiral Raeder as head of the Kriegsmarine, the service's emphasis on the surface fleet changed dramatically in favour of submarine warfare, and by the beginning of 1943 the aircraft carrier - and its aircraft - were once again no longer a priority.

Newly-built Ju 87G-2 at the factory. Note that anti-tank guns have yet to be mounted.

R. Michulec.

Junkers Ju 87G

The dive bomber as a weapon of war was becoming a thing of the past, and following the multi-role Ju 87D, only one more model followed which was the highly specialised, tank-busting G model. The idea of aircraft carrying large calibre guns of sufficient 'punch' to inflict severe damage to tanks was gaining currency, and the Allies had already developed aircraft of this type - notably the Hawker Hurricane Mk IID which had appeared in March 1942 armed with two 40mm Vickers S guns. In autumn of that year the RLM decided to trial aircraft armed with the 37mm Flak 18 anti-tank cannon, and selected the Messerchmitt Bf 110, Junkers Ju 88, Henschel Hs 129 and Junkers Ju 87. The three twin-engined types could be fitted with a single cannon in a belly-mounted pod, but the single-engine layout of the Ju 87 precluded this solution. The only alternative was to carry two of the weapons, one under each wing, despite the fact that they each weighed 270 kg (594 lb) 'dry', without ammunition or auxiliary equipment, and 425 kg (935 lb) all-up. This meant that the pilot had to manage the equivalent of

Detail shot of Ju 87G's 37mm Flak 18 anti-tank cannon.
Stratus coll.

Ju 87G-1 of 'Panzerjagdkommando Weiss".
via R. Michulec.

Field calibration of Flak 18 cannon.

via R. Michulec.

not only taking off and flying, but also landing with two heavy bombs under each wing.

Stuka Ju 87 D-1, W.Nr. 2552, served as the prototype for the Ju 87G (informally known as 'Gustav') and during the tests drew favourable comments despite its added weight. The Ju 87G proved more demanding than standard Stukas, but provided it was flown by experienced pilots, this was acceptable to the *Luftwaffe* for the relatively small number of aircraft that would be required. Following the trials, the prototype G model and some machines from the first production batch were sent to the front for field trials. A special unit was formed for this purpose called the *Versuchsverband* fur *Panzerkampfung* (anti tank trials unit), which was colloquially known as *Kommando Weiß* after its commander, Obstlt. Otto Weiß.

Ju 87G-2.

Stratus coll.

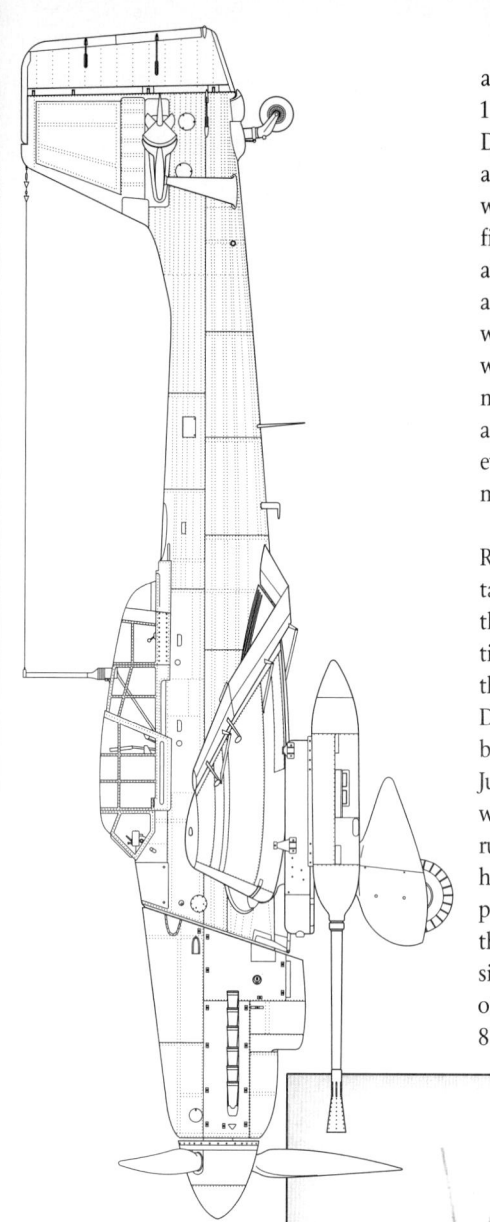

The machines went into action around February 1943 and the first combat losses were recorded on the 18th and 19th March 1943 when W.Nr. 1097, DJ+FT and W.Nr. 1132, DJ+JE, were shot down. During this period the strengths and weaknesses of the Ju 87G were made apparent. As was found in the state trials, the G model was more difficult to fly than a standard Stuka and more vulnerable to attack - a standard aircraft could at least jettison its bombs and run, which the tank busting Stukas could not. The weight and drag of the cannon eroded the Ju 87G's speed, which was never high anyway. The cannon also affected manoeuvrability and handling, especially at low speeds, and despite recoil mechanisms and blast tubes, the effect every time the cannon fired was severe. All other wing mounted guns were deleted.

Nevertheless, many pilots liked the Ju 87G, and the RLM and test facility at Rechlin also favoured the Stuka tank buster over the twin engined Hs 129 and Bf 110, as the twin guns of the Ju 87 offered better chances of hitting the target. Therefore, 208 Ju 87Gs were ordered. Of these, there were 34 Ju 87G-1s which were based on the D-1 and D-3, and the rest were built as G-2s which were based on the Ju 87D-5 airframe with its longer wings. The Ju 87G production was relatively small and therefore there were few developments introduced during the production run. However, some aircraft built near the end of the war had 20 mm cannon added within the wing as well as the podded 37 mm below, making for what must have been the heaviest forward facing gun armament carried by any single-engine aircraft in the Second World War. By the end of the war, the tank-busting Staffel of III/SG 2 had 21 Ju 87G-2s on strength.

Ju 87G-1.
1/72 scale.

Ju 87G-2.

Stratus coll.

Junkers Ju 87H

A dedicated pilot trainer version of the Stuka was the last in the alphanumeric sequence of Ju 87s. Like the tank-busting G model, the Ju 87H was derived from production D models and it is likely that there were five versions, H-1, H-3, H-5, H-7 and H-8, depending on the original specification of the D model that was converted - the latter two may have been trainers that were converted from D-1s and D-3s fitted with the D-5 wing during overhauls, for example.

The trainer version of the Stuka had dual controls which were taken from the Arado Ar 96. The rear cockpit was consequently completely redesigned with a taller rear canopy to allow the pilot in the aft seat to sit higher.

It is estimated that only around 50 Ju 87 trainers were completed.

Ju 87H-3. 1/72 scale.

Uncompleted developments: Ju 87F, Ju 187 & Ju 287.

A successor to the Ju 87D was planned from spring 1941, even before that model had gone into production. As with previous developments, the improved model, designated the Ju 87F, was based around a more powerful Jumo engine, the 1,750 PS(1,725 hp) D 213A. However, the larger, heavier and more powerful engine created substantial problems with installation into the Ju 87 airframe which required a great deal of alteration. Nevertheless Junkers persevered with the developments, which also included a new wing that could be equipped with the MG 151/20 and MG 131 cannon.

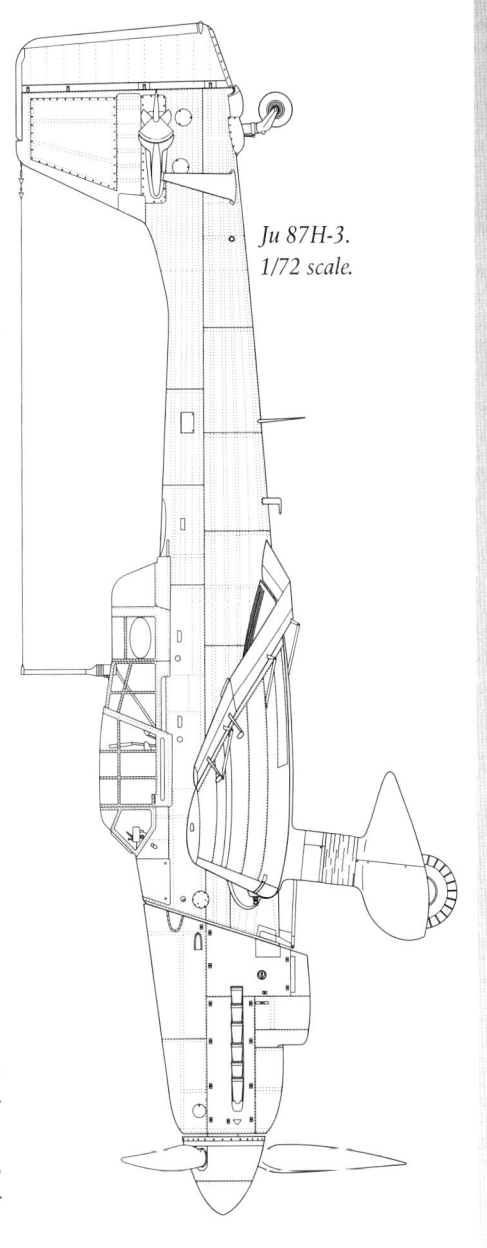

However, in 1943 the Ju 87F project was shelved in favour of a substantially different aircraft, the Ju 187. Though this shared a similar layout with the Ju 87F, the airframe was to be completely new with some innovative features such as a tail that could revolve to clear the gunner's field of fire. Work on this project began in the summer of 1943. However, the Ju 187 was of low priority with the need to use the maximum capacity in the aircraft industry to produce fighters, and this eventually caused the cancellation of the Ju 187. A further development, which looked even less like the original Stuka, the Ju 287, was similarly short lived. (See the MMP book *German Air Projects 1935 – 1945 vol.3: Bombers* for further details.)

Different engines were also considered as a means of developing the Ju 87, including the Daimler Benz DB 605. This engine was in great demand for fighters which were given priority and could therefore not be spared for dive bombers.

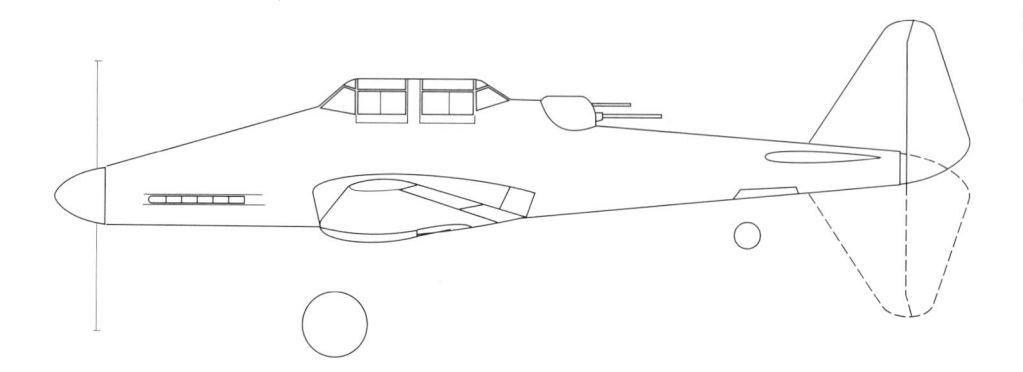

*Ju 187.
Not to scale.*

Junkers Ju 87 Production

The exact number of Junkers Ju 87s built is not certain, but the generally accepted figure is 5,709 of all types. This includes 262 Ju 87As, 922 Ju 87Bs, 721 Ju 87Rs, 3537 Ju 87Ds, 208 Ju 87Gs and a further 59 machines of unkown type which probably include Ju 87H trainers, and some prototype and pre-production machines.

However, there is some contradiction in contemporary documents which means it is impossible to be certain what the precise production figures are. For example, the monthly returns for 1944 state that 849 Ju 87s were built, while summarised data suggests that 1,012 were completed. The Weserflug factory data suggests 771 Ju 87s produced by that company in 1944.

Technical Data

	Ju 87 A-1		Ju 87 B-1		Ju 87 B-2		Ju 87 R-2		Ju 87 C-1	
Wing span	13.60 m	44.61 ft	13.80 m	45.27 ft	13.60 m	44.61 ft	13.60 m	44.61 ft	13.20 m	43.30 ft
Length	10.78 m	35.36 ft	11.10 m	36.41 ft	11.10 m	36.41 ft	11.10 m	36.41 ft	11.00 m	36.08 ft
Heigh	3.89 m	12.76 ft	4.01 m	13.15 ft	4.01 m	13.15 ft	4.01 m	13.15 ft	3,77	12,36 ft
Wing area	31.90 m²	343.97 sq.ft	31.90 m²	343.97 sq.ft	31.90 m²	343.97 sq.ft	31.90 m²	343.97 sq.ft	31.30 m²	336.92 sq.ft
Wing area load	106.6 kg/m²	21.83 lb/sq f.	136 kg/m²	27.85 lb/sq ft	136 kg/m²	27.85 lb/sq ft	177,2 kg/m²	36,27 lb/m²	141 kg/m²	28.87 lb/sq ft
Wright empty	2300 kg	5070.63 lb	2710 kg	5974.53 lb	2750 kg	6062.71 lb	2750 kg	6062.71 lb	2900 kg	6393.41 lb
Wright take off	3400 kg	7495.72 lb	4250 kg	9369.65 lb	4250 kg	9369.65 lb	4350 kg	9590.11 lb	4510 kg	9942.85 lb
Engine	Jumo 210D		Jumo 211 A-1		Jumo 211 Da		Jumo 211 Da		Jumo 211 Da	
Power max	500kW (680KM)	670.51 hp	736 kW (1000 KM)	986.99 hp	883 kW (1200 KM)	1184.12 hp	883 kW (1200 KM)	1184.12 hp	883 kW (1200 KM)	1184.12 hp
Propeller	Jumo Hamilton HPA		Jumo Hamilton HPA III		VS 5 (later VS 11)		VS 11		Jumo Hamilton	
Max Speed	320 km/h	199 mph	383 km/h	238 mph	380km/h	236 mph	340 km/h	211 mph	380 km/h	236 mph
At	4000 m	13 123 ft	4100 m	13451 ft	4100 m	13451 ft	0 m	0 ft	4100 m	13451 ft
Cruise Speer	275 km/h	171 mph	336 km/h	209 mph	336 km/h	209 mph	280 km/h	174 mph	306 km/h	190 mph
At	2700 m	8858 ft	3700 m	12139 ft	3700 m	12139 ft	4600 m	15092 ft	5000 m	16404 ft
Landing Speed	100 km/h	62 mph	108 km/h	67 mph	108 km/h	67 mph	130 km/h	81 mph	100 km/h	62 mph
Max diving speed	450 km/h	280 mph	650 km/h	404 mph	650 km/h	404 mph	650 km/h	404 mph	650 km/h	404 mph
Time of reach	3000 m 23 min	9843 ft 23 min	4000 m 12 min	13123 ft 12 min	4000 m 12 min	13123 ft 12 min	NO DATA		3000 m 13.36 min	9843 ft 13.36 min
Ceiling	7000 m	22966 ft	8000 m	26247 ft	8000 m	26247 ft	7000 m	22966 ft	8000 m	26247 ft
Range normal	NO DATA		600 km	373 miles	600 km	373 miles	NO DATA		NO DATA	
Range max	1000 km	621 miles	790 km	491 miles	790 km	491 miles	1450 km	901 miles	1160 km	721 miles
Armament	1 MG 17 / 7.9 mm		2 MG 17 / 7.9 mm		2 MG 17 / 7.9 mm		2 MG 17 / 7.9 mm		2 MG 17 / 7.9 mm	
(defence)	1 MG 15 / 7.9 mm		1 MG 15 / 7.9 mm		1 MG 15 / 7.9 mm		1 MG 81 Z / 7.9 mm		1 MG 15 / 7.9 mm	
Bombs	250 kg	551 lb	500 kg	1102 lb	700 kg	1543 lb	500 kg	1102 lb	700 kg	1543 lb

Remarks:
1- With one crew and 500 kg / 1102 lb bombs

Junkers Ju 87 "STUKA"

	Ju 87 D-1		Ju 87 D-5		Ju 87 D-8		Ju 87 G-2		Ju 87 H-1	
Wing span	13.60 m	44.61 ft	14.98 m	49.14 ft	14.98 m	49.14 ft	14.98 m	49.14 ft	14.98 m	49.14 ft
Length	11.50 m	37.73 ft	11.50 m	37.73 ft	11.50 m	37.73 ft	11.50 m	37.73 ft	11.50 m	37.73 ft
Heigh	3.88 m	12.73 ft	3.88 m	12.73 ft	3.88 m	12.73 ft	3.88 m	12.73 ft	3.88 m	12.73 ft
Wing area	31.90 m^2	343.97 sq.ft	33.68 m^2	362.54 sq.ft	33.68 m^2	362.54 sq.ft	33.68 m^2	362.54 sq.ft	33.68 m^2	362.54 sq.ft
Wing area load	206.9 kg/m^2	42.37 lb/sq ft	196kg/m^2	40.14 lb/sq ft	197 kg/m^2	40.35 lb/sq ft	195 kg/m^2	30.94 lb/sq ft	156.1 kg/m^2	31,97lb/sq ft
Wight empty	3900 kg	8598.03 lb	3940 kg	8686.22 lb	3938 kg	8681.81 lb	3930 kg	8664,17 lb	NO DATA	
Wight take off	6600 kg	14550 lb	6580 kg	14506 lb	6607 kg	14566 lb	5960 kg	13140 lb	5000 kg	11023 lb
Engine	Jumo 211 J-1		Jumo 211 J-1		Jumo 211 P		Jumo 211 J-1		Jumo 211 J-1	
Power max	1044kW	1400 hp	1044kW	1400 hp	1104 kW	1480 hp	1044 kW	1400 hp	1044 kW	1400 hp
	1420 KM		(1420 KM)		(1500 KM)		(1420 KM)		(1420 KM)	
Propeller	VS 11		VS 11		VS 11		VS 11		VS 11	
Max speed	410 km/h	255 mph	400 km/h	249 mph	400 km/h	249 mph	396 km/h	246 mph	410 km/h	255 mph
At	4100 m	13451 ft	4100 m	13451 ft	4400 m	14436 ft	4000 m	13123 ft	4100 m	13451 ft
Cruise speed	310 km/h	193 mph	318 km/h	198 mph	310 km/h	193 mph	326 km/h	203 mph	370 km/h	230 mph
At	5100 m	16732 ft	5000 m	16404 ft	5000 m	16404 ft	5000 m	16404 ft	5000 m	/16404 ft
Landing Speed	110 km/h	68 mph	110 km/h	68 mph	110 km/h	68 mph	120 km/h	75 mph	110 km/h	68 mph
Max diving speed	650 km/h	404 mph	650 km/h	404 mph	NO DATA		NO DATA		NO DATA	
Time to reach	5000 m	16404 ft	5000 m	16404 ft	5000 m	16404 ft			3000 m	9843 ft
	19 min		20 min		20 min				13.36 min	13.36 min
Ceiling	7285 m	23900 ft	7500 m	24606 ft	7500 m	24606 ft	7360 m	24147 ft	8100 m	26575 ft
Range normal	NO DATA		NO DATA		NO DATA		600 km	373 miles	NO DATA	
Range max	1535 km	954 miles	1530 km	951 miles	1535 km	954 miles	1530 km	951 miles	1000 km	621 miles
Armament	2 MG 17 / 7.9 mm		2 MG 151/20, 20 mm		2 MG 151/20, 20 mm		2 BK 37 / 37 mm		2 MG 17 / 7.9 mm	
(defence)	1 MG 81 Z / 7.9 mm		1 MG 81 Z / 7.9 mm		1 MG 81 Z / 7.9 mm		1 MG 81 Z / 7.9 mm			
Bombs	1000 kg	2205 lb	1000 kg	2205 lb	1000 kg	2205 lb				

Detail photos Ju 87A

Junkers Ju 87 "STUKA"

A damaged photograph of a Ju 87A in pre-war camouflage scheme.
Stratus coll.

Starboard view of Ju 87A-2.
Stratus coll.

67

Starboard side of the Ju 87A-2 cowling. Note the unidentified fairing under the fuselage.
via R. Michulec.

Right: *Engine cowling of Ju 87A.*
Drawing from Technical Manual.

Below: *Side view of the Ju 87A portside.*
Stratus coll.

Three photos of Ju 87A models on the assembly line. The bottom image shows the underside of the (inverted) fuselage centre section.

via R. Michulec.

69

Two photos of Ju 87A engine details. **Stratus coll.**

Port side of Jumo 210 Da engine.
> **Technical Manual.**

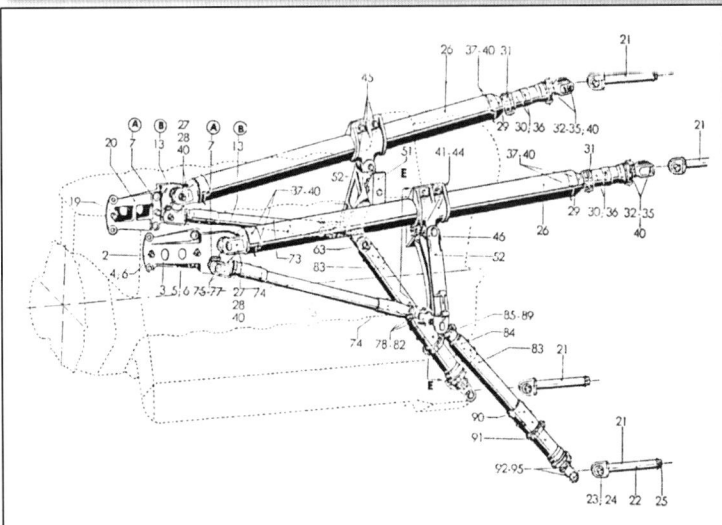

Engine mount of Jumo 210 Da.
> **Technical Manual**

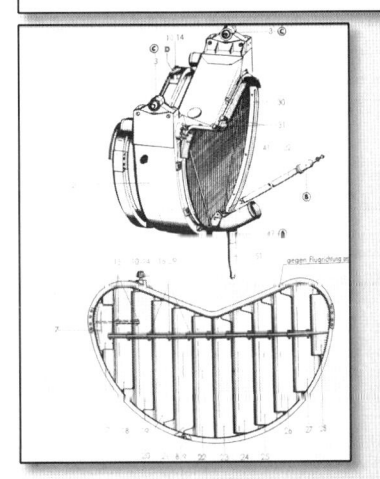

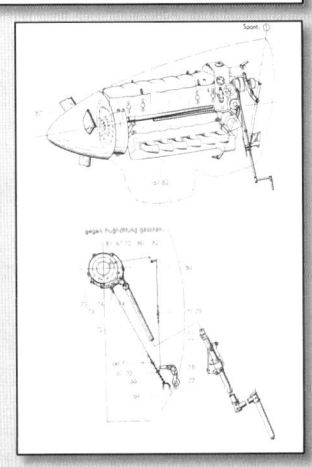

Bottom, left: Details of the engine coolant radiator.

Bottom, right: Engine starter crank.
> **Technical Manual**

Junkers Ju 87 "STUKA"

Ju 87A wing structure shown during aircraft assembly.
via R. Michulec.

Below: Details of the starboard undercarriage.

Bottom: Drawings showing the bomb support for 250 kg (left) and 500 kg (right) bombs.
Technical Manual.

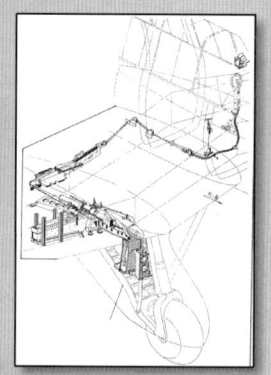

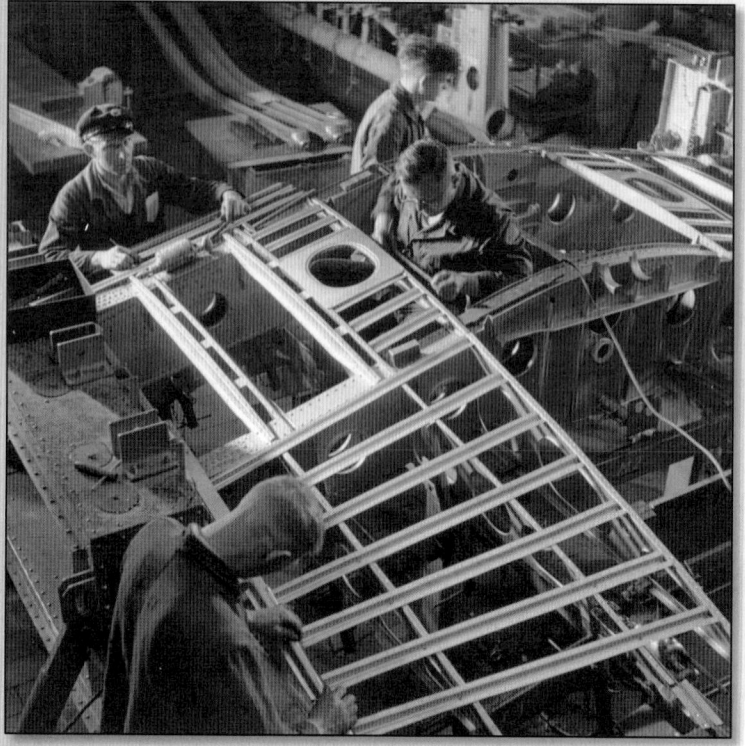

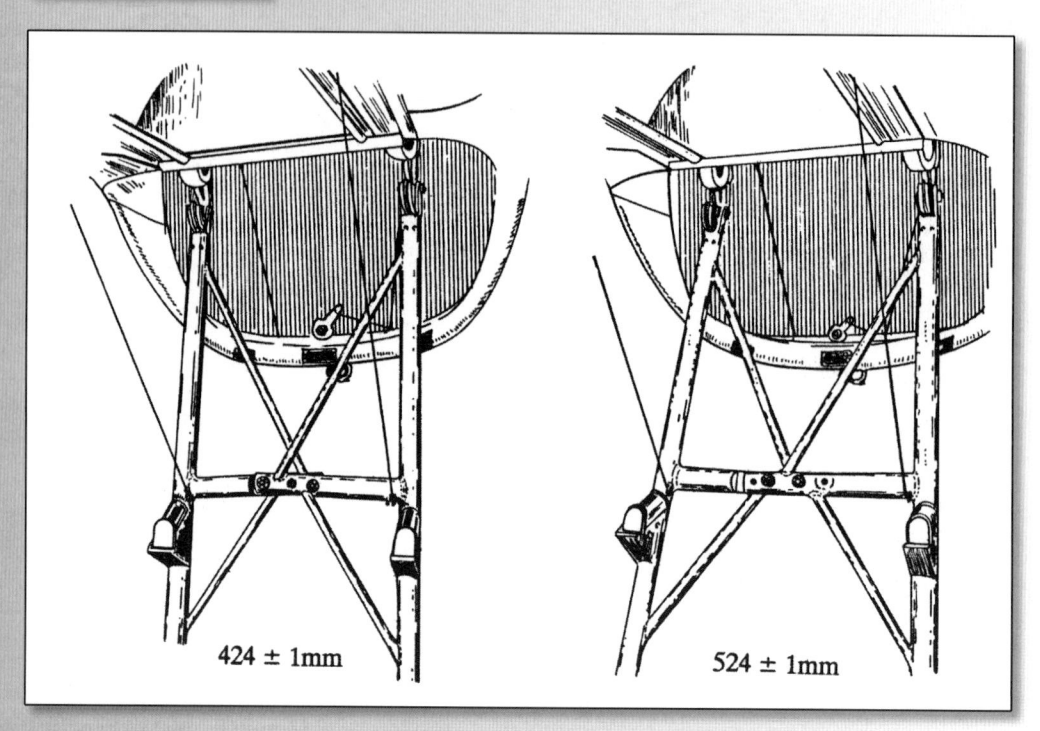

424 ± 1mm

524 ± 1mm

Above: Details of Ju 87A fin and rudder construction. **Technical Manual**
Left: Details of Ju 87A bomb support. Note also the undercarriage struts.
Stratus coll.
Below: Tail wheel details. **Technical Manual.**

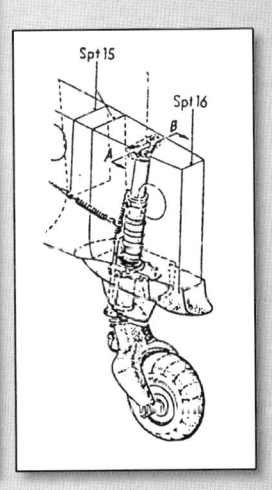

Junkers Ju 87 "STUKA"

Rear cockpit details.
Technical Manual.

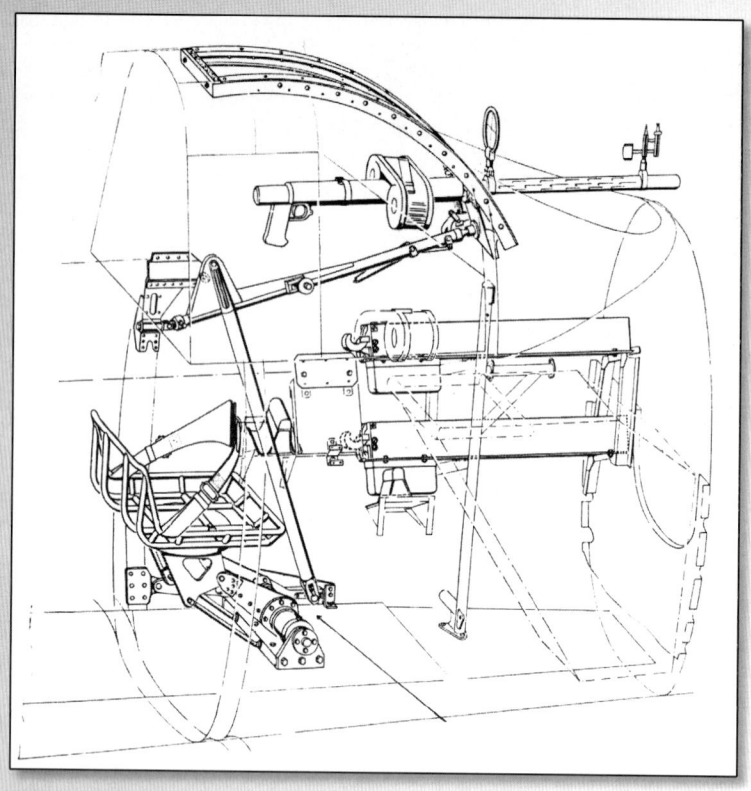

Two photos of Ju 87A canopy.
Stratus coll.

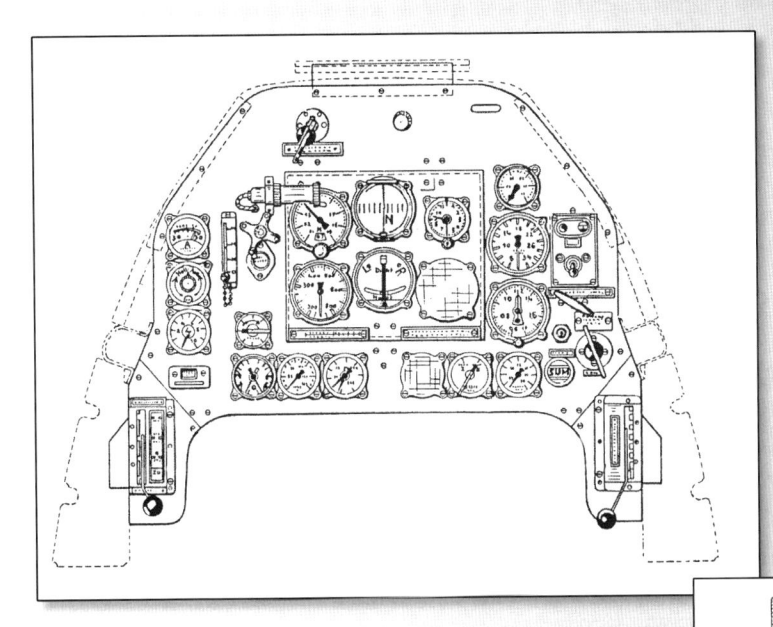

Ju 87A instrument panel.
Technical Manual

Side view of the rudder pedals, Ju 87A.
Technical Manual.

Fuselage of Ju 87A awaiting its engine on the production line.
via R. Michulec.

Junkers Ju 87 "STUKA"

75

Junkers Ju 87 "STUKA"

Ju 87B

Portside of the Ju 87B-1 nose. Aircraft of III./St.G 51, France 1940. **M. Griehl.**

A pair of Ju 87B-1 of 12(St.)/LG 1, France 1940. **via P. Smith.**

Ju 87B fuselages on factory line.
Stratus coll.

Below: Ju 87B-1 W.Nr. 435 6G+LS of St.G 51. Note details of the rear fuselage.
Stratus coll.

Front part of the Ju 87B-1 (late) fuselage. Note that sirens are removed.
Stratus coll.

Rear view of the Ju 87B-1, W.Nr. 429 of 3./St.G 2, spring 1940.
via R. Michulec.

Right: A pair of Ju 87B of St.G 51, in flight. Aircraft in winter camouflage.

Below: Ju 87B-1 (early) on the way back from a mission.
via R. Michulec.

Close up photo of Ju 87B of I./St.G 2, Balkans, spring 1941. Note the gun camera in the starboard wing.
via P. Smith.

Left: Ju 87B-1 (early) of I./St.G 1.
Stratus coll.

Below: Front view of Ju 87B-1.
via R. Michulec.

Junkers Ju 87 "STUKA"

79

Junkers Ju 87 "STUKA"

Three photos of a Ju 87 releasing a bomb in the dive.

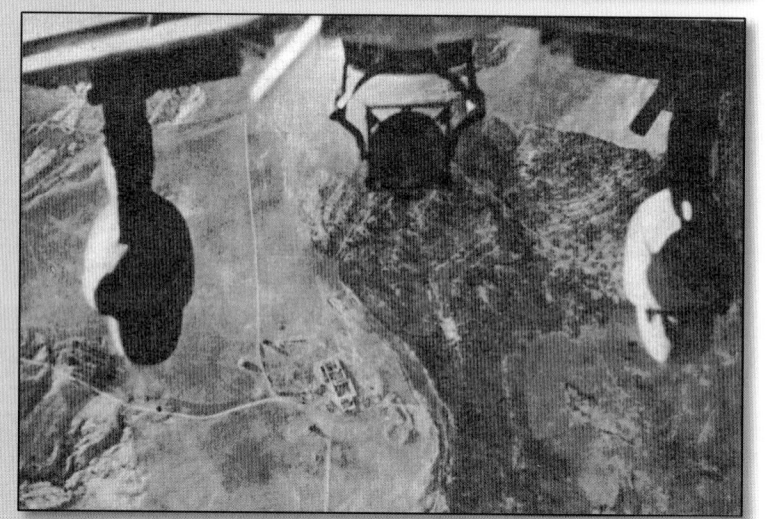

Stratus coll.

Ju 87R-2 of the **Afrika Korps** on display of Museum Of Science and Technology, Chicago. This aircraft was registered A5+HL and was captured by British Forces in Libya in 1941. The aircraft was transferred to the USA and displayed in Chicago's Museum of Science and Industry. Later it was restored and shown at the EAA Air Museum in Hales Corners, before it was moved back to its present location in Chicago. **M. Shreeve.** The black and white photo shows the aircraft in the mid-1940s, and clearly shows what was still attached (and thus is original in today's colour photographs) and also therefore what has been replaced since this picture. The one replacement item known of in this picture is the wheels, believed to be from a T-6. S. Tournay coll.

Junkers Ju 87 "STUKA"

This and opposite page: : The Ju 87 R-2 on display of Museum Of Science and Technology, Chicago. The paint is believed to be almost all original (with some touch-ups and repairs). The upper colours are the standard RLM 79 sandy brown with RLM 80 olive blotches. The undersides are RLM 78 sky blue, but the original (lighter and greener) RLM 65 light blue can be seen around the stencilling, which was masked off when the tropical colours were applied. M. Shreeve.

Detail shot of the Ju 87R-2 tail and wing bomb racks.

Beata & Michał

Port view of Ju 87B-1, (late).

Stratus coll.

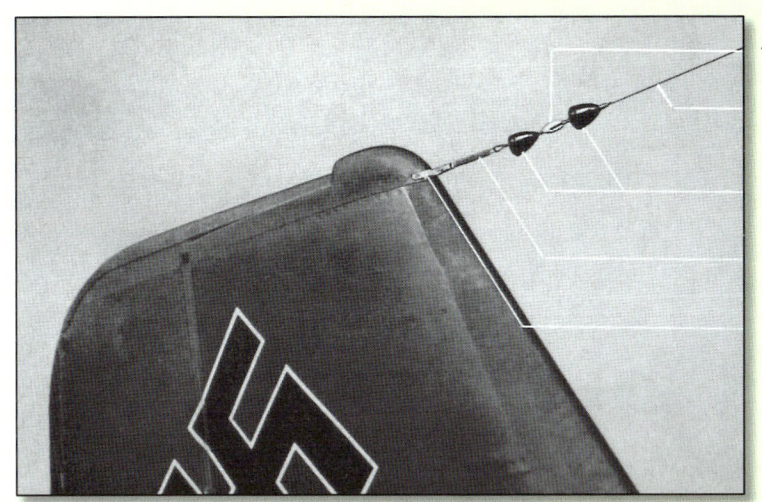

*Ju 87B tail fin.
Photo from Technical Manual.*

*Starboard side of the rear part of Ju 87R-2 fuselage.
Beuła & Michał*

*Underside of Ju 87R-2.
M. Shreeve.*

Ju 87B during engine maintenance.
　　　　　via R. Michulec.

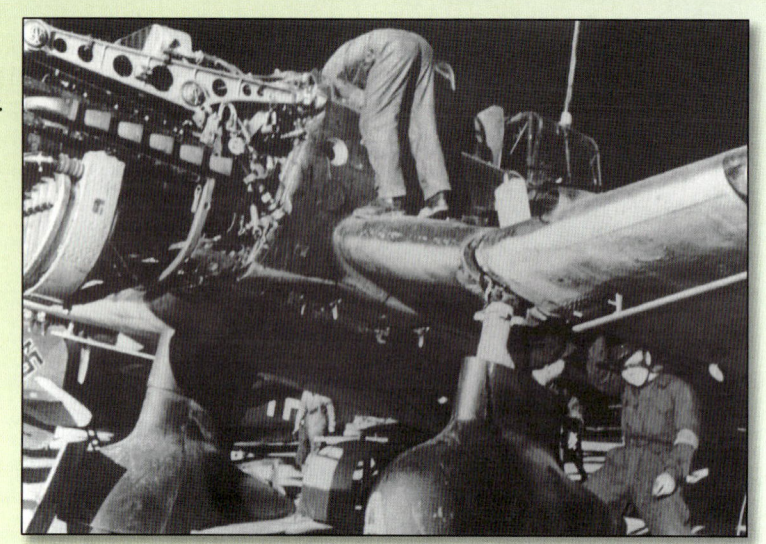

Two photos of a Jumo 211 A engine preserved at Muzeum Lotnictwa Polskiego (MLP) in Krakow, Poland.
　　　　　R. Panek.

The port side of the Jumo 211 A engine, preserved in MLP, Kraków.
R. Panek.

Ju 87B with engine cowling removed. Engine mount and radiator are clearly visible.
Stratus coll.

Junkers Ju 87 "STUKA"

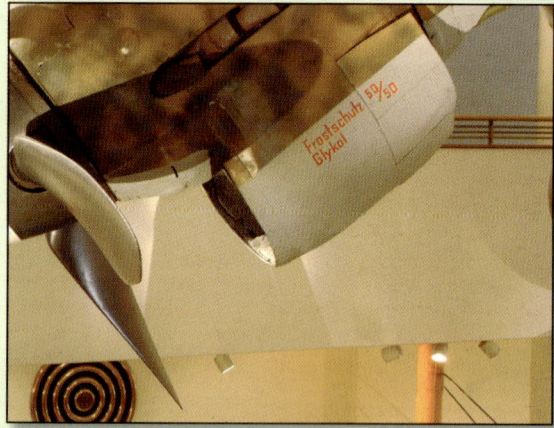

Above: Front view of Ju 87B-1 radiator.
Stratus coll.
Left: Two photos of Ju 87B radiator.
Beata & Michał.
Below: Starboard side of the Ju 87R-2 nose. The tropical filter is visible. *M. Shreeve.*

Starboard side of the Ju 87R-2 radiator. The tropical filter is also visible. Note details of the undercarriage.
Beata & Michał.

A Ju 87B engine with upper cowlings removed, showing the engine bearers.
Stratus coll.

Starboard side of a Ju 87R engine with lower cowlings removed and radiator visible.
Stratus coll.

Above: Port side of Ju 87R canopy. **M. Shreeve.**
Below: Rear part of the Ju 87B canopy. Note that part of the framing is inside the canopy. **Stratus coll.**

Above: The centre part of the canopy with antenna mount.
Technical Manual.
Right: The rear, moveable part of Ju 87B canopy.
Stratus coll.
Below: The front part of the Ju 87B/R canopy.
Beata & Michał.

Junkers Ju 87 "STUKA"

Rear part of the Ju 87B canopy.
Stratus coll.

Below: Drawing of the Ju 87B canopy. Technical Manual.

Bottom: Close up view of the Ju 87B rear canopy and gunner's machine gun.
Stratus coll.

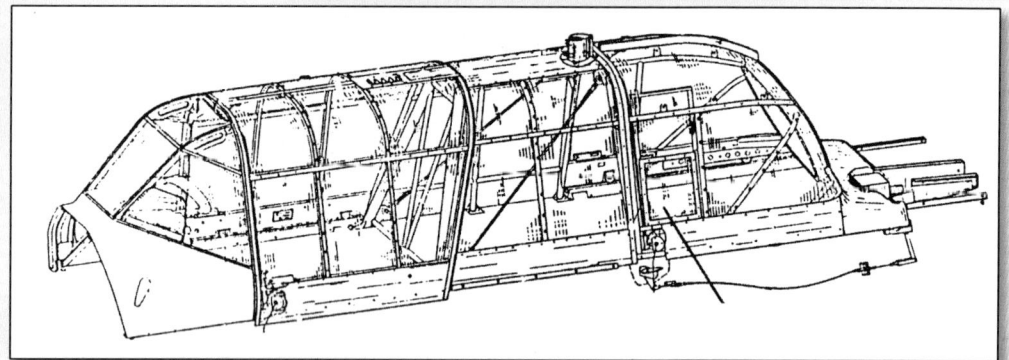

Above: Rear view of the Ju 87B gunner's position. **Stratus coll.**

Starboard side of the Ju 87R-2 canopy.

Beata & Michał.

Junkers Ju 87 "STUKA"

Ju 87B-1/R-1 instrument panel.
Technical Manual.

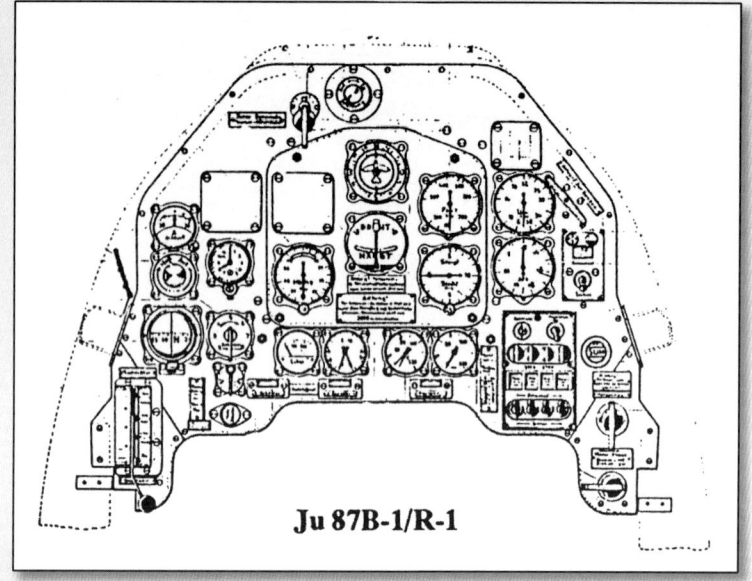

Photo of the rear Ju 87B cockpit, looking from the portside, aft.
Technical Manual.

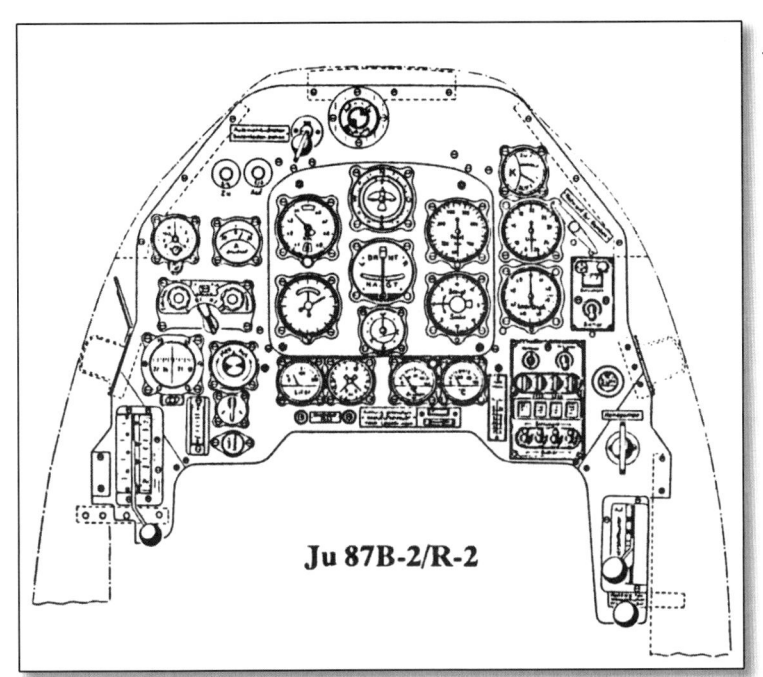

Ju 87B-2/R-2 instrument panel.
   Technical Manual.

Ju 87B-2/R-2

Abb.1: Führerraum, linke Rumpfseitenwand, quer gegen Flugrichtung gesehen

Flugrichtung

⑯ Telefonieverstärker TV. 1a
⑰ Umformer UTV. 24
⑲ Anschlußdose ADb. 9

⑩ Schwingungsanzeiger SchA. 5a
⑮ₐ LK. II F 18 für Antennenleitung
⑯ Telefonieverstärker
⑰ Umformer für Telefonieverstärker UTV. 24
⑥ Sender S. 6b
⑦ Empfänger E. 5a
Leitung 17 F
⑧ₐ Leitungskupplung LK. II F 18 für Erdleitung

Two photos from the Technical Manual showing the rear (gunner's) cockpit. The lower photo shows the radio gear.
   Technical Manual.

Junkers Ju 87 "STUKA"

95

Junkers Ju 87 "STUKA"

Ju 87B wing, underside. Note that landing flaps and aileron are removed. Stratus coll.

Underside of the preserved Ju 87R-2.
M. Shreeve.

Three photos of underwing details.
Bomb racks and aileron controls.

Beata & Michał.

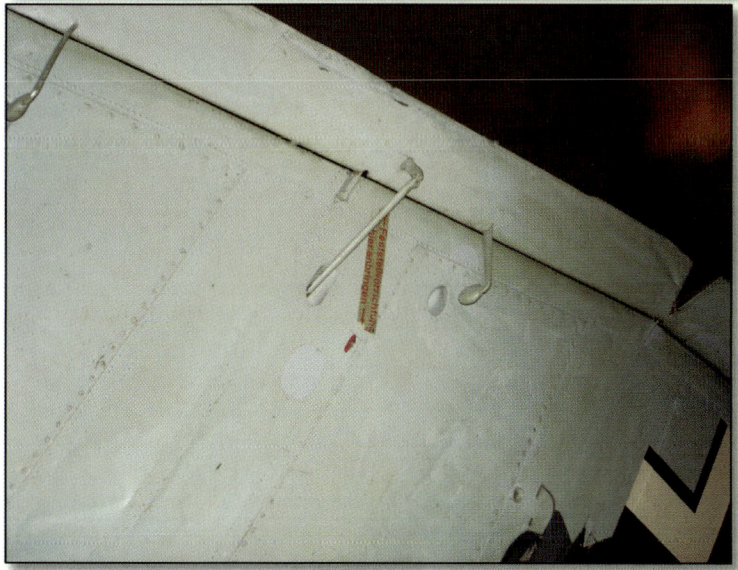

Junkers Ju 87 "STUKA"

*Underwing details.
Beata & Michał.*

98

Upper part of the starboard wing.
Beata & Michał.

Junkers Ju 87 "STUKA"

Details of Ju 87B/R type undercarriage with spats and brakelines removed.
Beata & Michał.

99

Junkers Ju 87 "STUKA"

Details of the wheel hub.
Beata & Michał.

Another shot of the Ju 87 B/R undercarriage.
M. Shreeve.

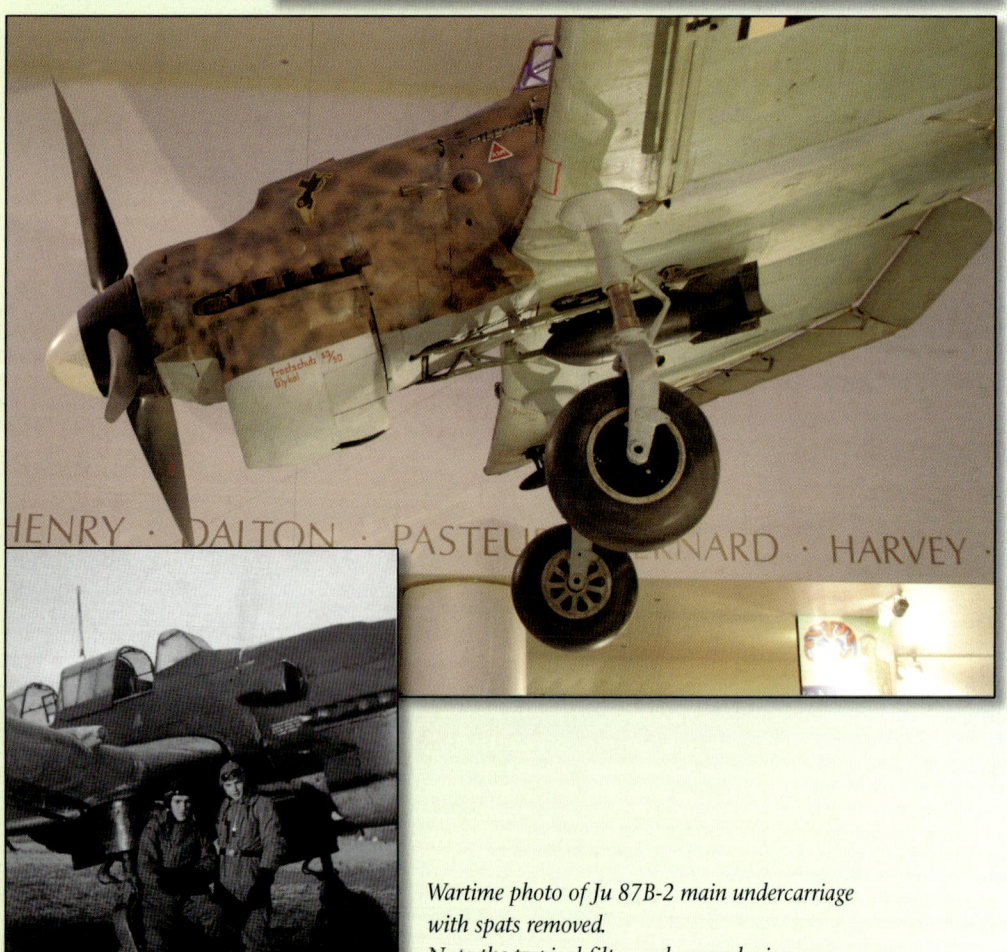

Wartime photo of Ju 87B-2 main undercarriage with spats removed. Note the tropical filter and covered wing gun.
Stratus coll.

100

Close up view of the port main undercarriage, Ju 87B.

Stratus coll.

Two photos of the Ju 87B-2 under preparation for another mission.

D. Bernád coll.

Junkers Ju 87 "STUKA"

Junkers Ju 87 "STUKA"

Ju 87D-G

Original wartime postcard of Ju 87D-5. Stratus coll.

The Stuka in the Battle of Britain Hall, RAF Museum, Hendon, UK. According to the official British records, this aircraft was built as Ju 87 D-3/trop, W.Nr. 2883, radio code "RI+JK". However this Stuka has the wings of of a D-5 and a VS 111 propeller. Also the dive brakes were removed and mounts for Flak18 37 mm cannon were added. All these parts are original, so it suggests that the aircraft was modified by the Germans to G-2 standard. The rear part of the canopy is not original. The rear machine gun, bomb release arm and the bomb itself are replicas.

R. Leigh.

Nose of a Ju 87D-1. Note the siren on the starboard undercarriage leg and early style exhaust, as well as the impact fuses on the wing bombs.
D. Bernád coll.

Preserved Ju 87D/G from the rear.
Stratus coll.

Junkers Ju 87 "STUKA"

Junkers Ju 87 "STUKA"

Port side of the Ju 87D/G at Hendon. *R. Leigh.*

Right: Starboard side of the Ju 87D/G fuselage. The last section of the canopy is not standard, having been modified during an attempted use in the 1960s Battle of Britain film. Gun is a wooden replica. **Stratus coll.**

Below: The RAF Museum's Ju 87 in 1969, still fitted with the mocked-up dive brakes, bomb-crutch and bomb and spat fitted sirens as prepared for the Battle of Britain film. An attempt was made to get the aircraft running, but not fully successfully, and the film used large scale models instead. **Ray Wood Collection, via Peter Arnold.**

104

Top: Port side of the canopy. Note non-standard sliding window.

Left & bottom: The last section of the canopy is not standard either. It could be a replica or a field modification. Gun is a wooden replica.

All photos Stratus coll.

Junkers Ju 87 "STUKA"

Rear part of the canopy from the right.

Port side of the canopy. The non-standard small sliding window is also visible.

Both photos Stratus coll.

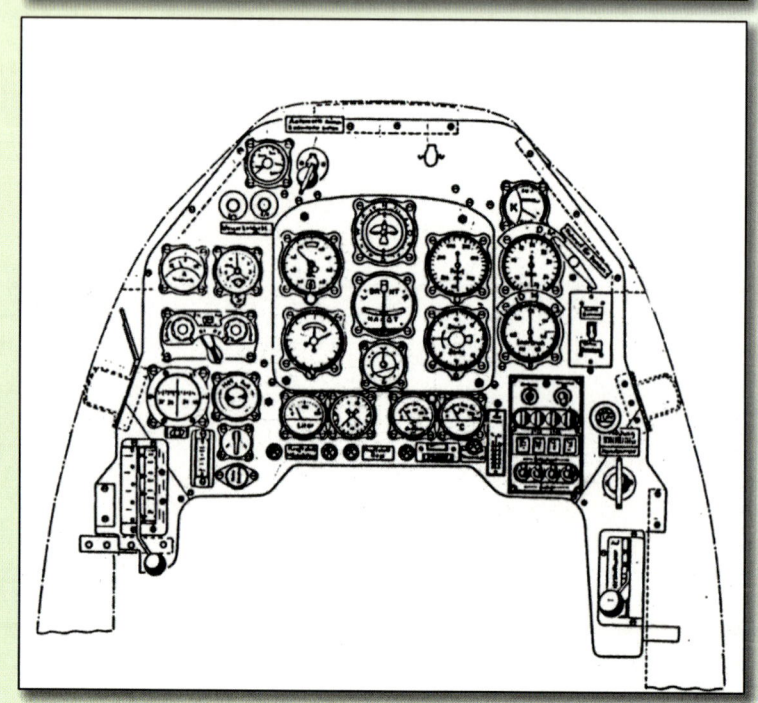

Ju 87D-3 instrument panel.
Technical Manual.

Above: The instrument panel of the Ju 87 preserved at Hendon. Some of the instruments have been lost.

Left: Port side of the front cockpit.

Bottom, left: Starboard side of the front cockpit.

Bottom, right: Pilot's seat from above.

All photos Stratus coll.

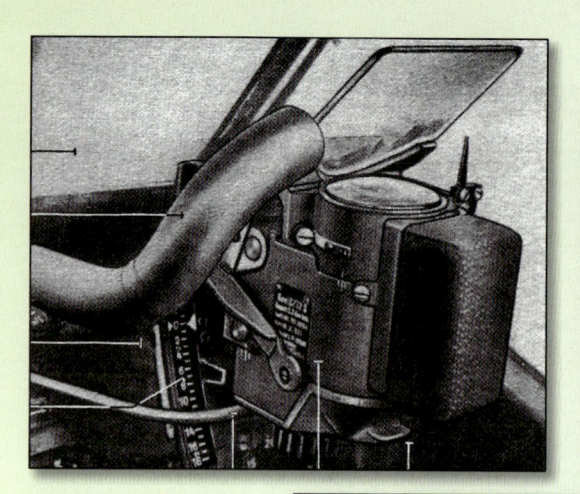

Junkers Ju 87 "STUKA"

Above, left: Revi C/12 D refelctor gunsight, as was used on Ju 87D.

Above right: Front cockpit, rear bulkhead.
   Photos from technical Manual.

Right: Starboard side of the canopy.
   Stratus coll.
Drawing of the rudder pedals, Ju 87D/G.
   Technical Manual.

Close up photo of the canopy.
   Stratus coll.

108

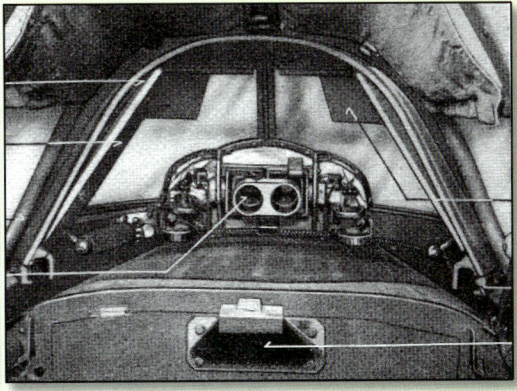

Above: Gunner's turret (GSL-k81Z) shown without machine guns. Technical Manual.

Above: Machine guns in the rear cockpit.
    Technical Manual.

Right: Pilot's and gunner's seats.
    Technical Manual.

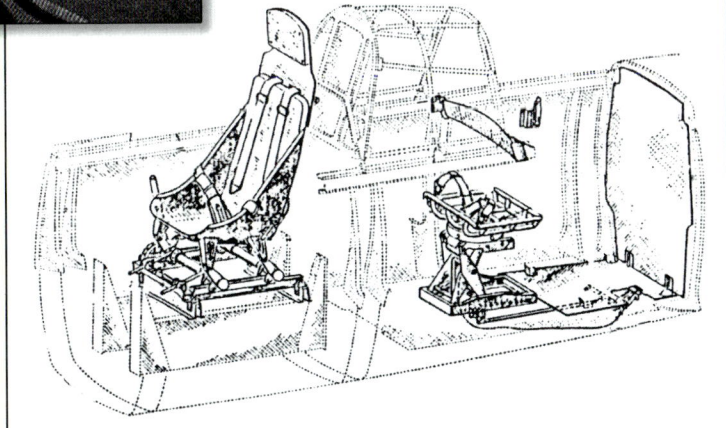

Port side of the third part of the canopy.
    Stratus coll.

Junkers Ju 87 "STUKA"

109

Front panel of the rear cockpit, just behind the pilot's seat. Above is the S6b radio transmitter, below is the F5a radio receiver.

Port side of the rear cockpit.

Another photo of the port side of the rear cockpit. The large box is the EZ4 direction-finding radio device.

All photos Stratus coll.

Starboard side of the engine cowling, Ju 87D/G.

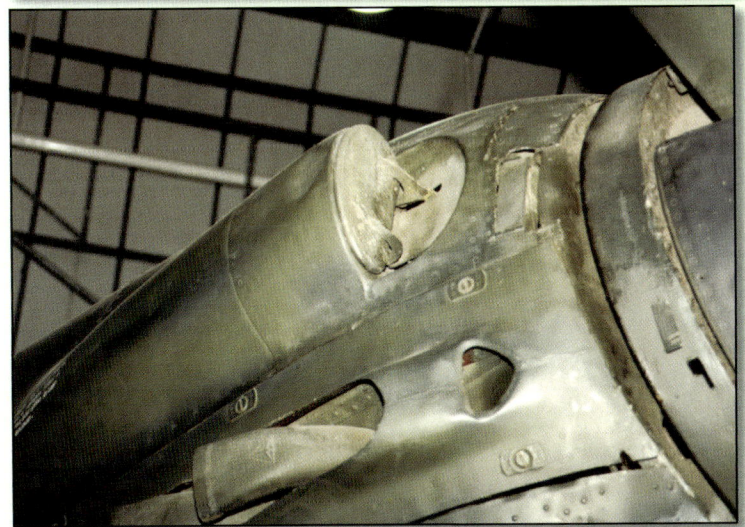

Details of the engine supercharger air intake with tropical filter. Note also details of the exhaust as was used on late D-3 and D-5.

Port side of the engine cowling. Details of the exhaust are visible.

All photos Stratus coll.

Junkers Ju 87 "STUKA"

Air, left and oil cooler, right, intakes.

Port side of the engine cowling.

Details of the Ju 87D/G exhaust pipes.
All photos Stratus coll.

Junkers Ju 87 "STUKA"

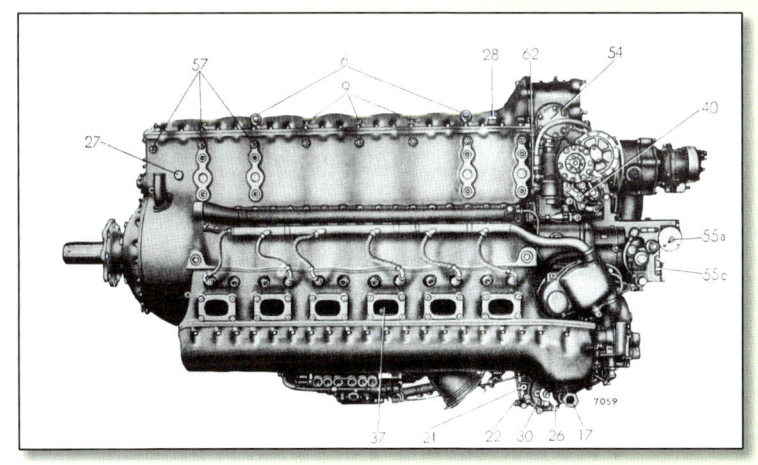

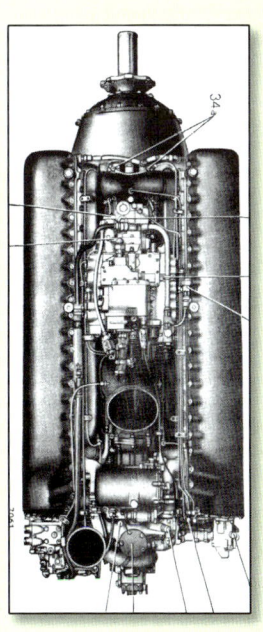

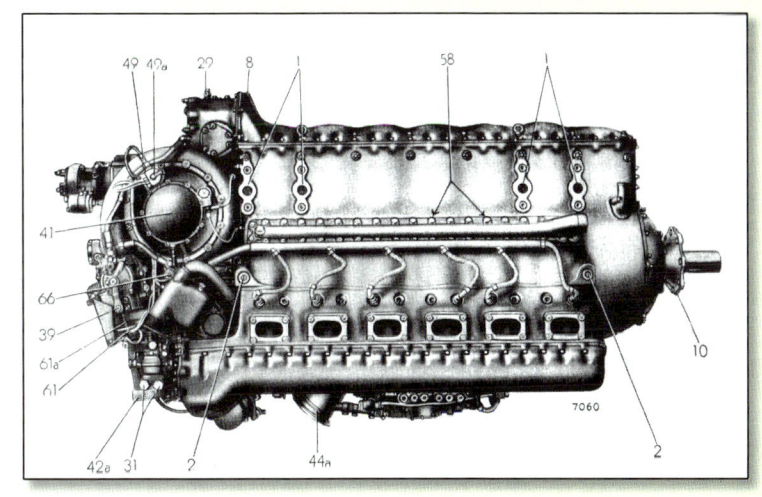

*This page:
Photos of Jumo 211 F/J engine.*

Technical Manual.

113

Port landing flap. Wing joint fairing is also visible.

Starboard, inner landing flap.

Engine cooler outlet, from rear.
All photos Stratus coll.

Front view of underwing radiator.

Side, outside view of the starboard underwing radiator.

Details of the flap control arm.
   All photos Stratus coll.

Flap and aileron controls.

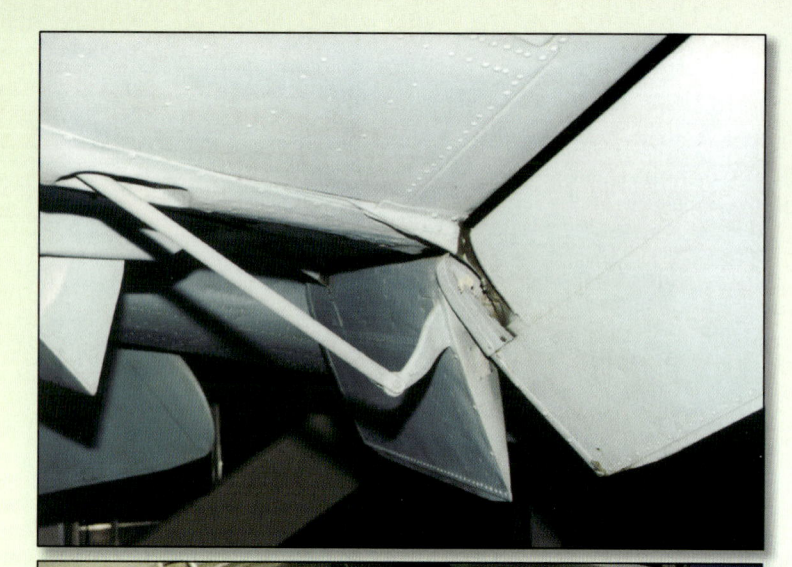

Upper surface of the port wing. The non-slip strips are visible.

Another view of the underwing radiator.
All photos Stratus coll.

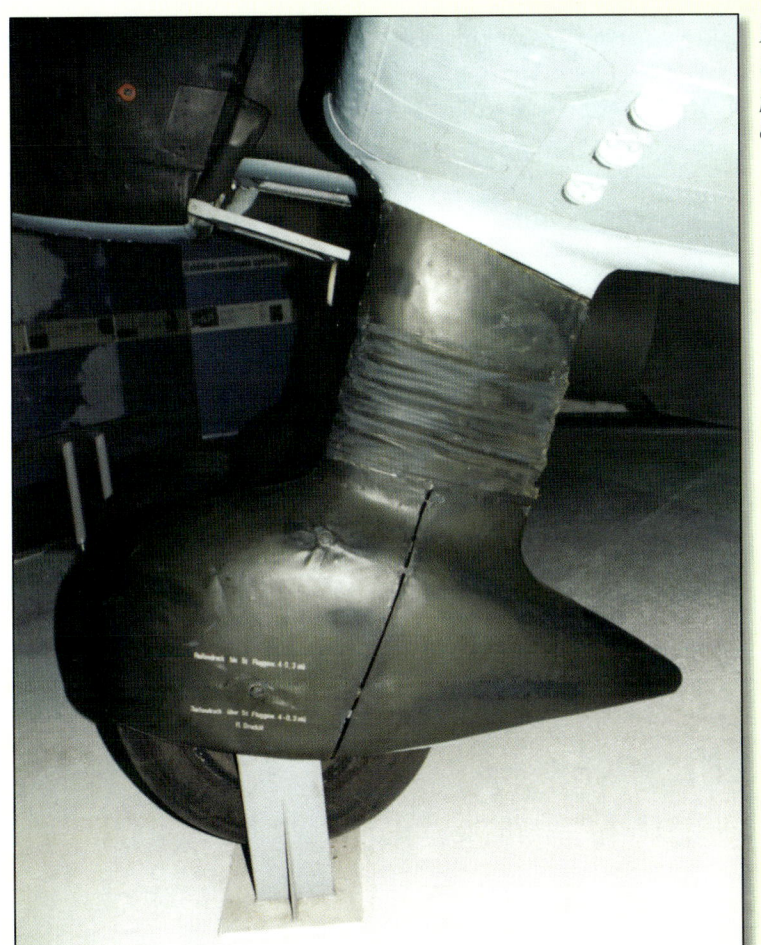

Port, main undercarriage leg. Note the mounting points of the 37mm BK cannon.

Undercarriage arrangement.

All photos Stratus coll.

Junkers Ju 87 "STUKA"

117

Junkers Ju 87 "STUKA"

Starboard, main undercarriage leg with spats removed.

Port undercarriage leg. Landing lamp is also visible.

All photos Stratus coll.

118

Two photos of Ju 87D/G tailwheel.

Port side of the rudder. Note the strut attachment points.
All photos Stratus coll.

Above: The starboard side of the tailplane. Details of the mass balance are visible.
Below: Starboard tailplane strut. **All photos Stratus coll.**

The starboard side of the Ju 87D/G nose. Note that bomb release arm and bomb itself are fakes. The arm is similar to that used on the Ju 87B.

Two photos of the bomb sighting window. Window shutter in open position.
All photos Stratus coll.

Junkers Ju 87 "STUKA"

121

Junkers Ju 87 "STUKA"

Drawing of MG151/20 cannons mounted into the Ju 87D-5 wing.
Technical Manual.

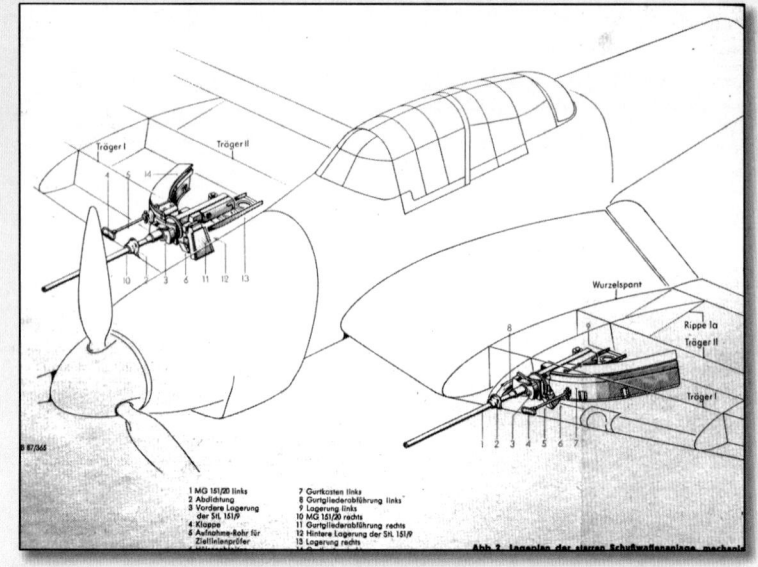

Photo of the cannon bay with cover removed, Ju 87D-5.
Technical Manual.

Detail photo of the gun cover in the wing root.
Technical Manual.

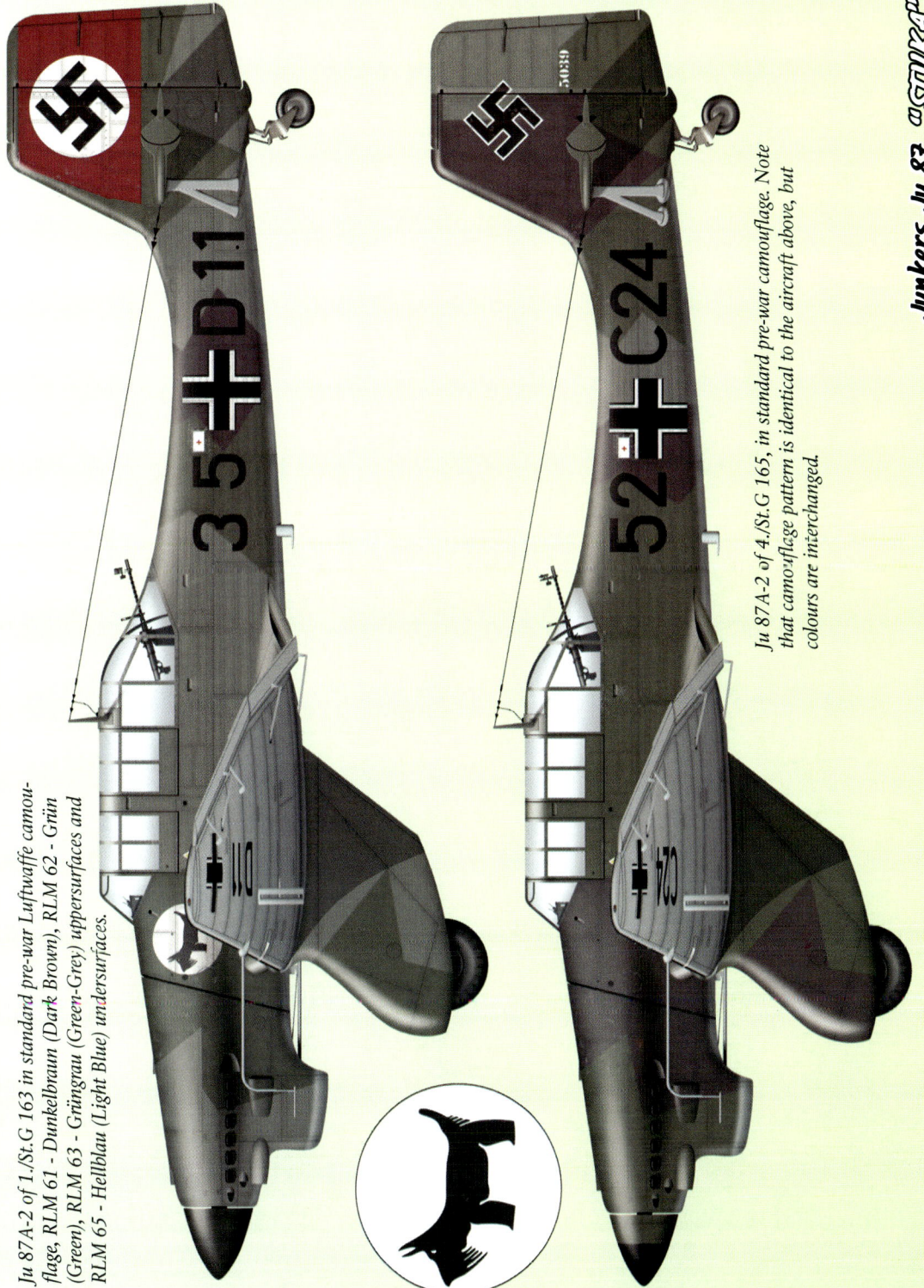

Ju 87A-2 of 1./St.G 163 in standard pre-war Luftwaffe camouflage, RLM 61 - Dunkelbraun (Dark Brown), RLM 62 - Grün (Green), RLM 63 - Grüngrau (Green-Grey) uppersurfaces and RLM 65 - Hellblau (Light Blue) undersurfaces.

Ju 87A-2 of 4./St.G 165, in standard pre-war camouflage. Note that camouflage pattern is identical to the aircraft above, but colours are interchanged.

Junkers Ju 87 "STUKA"

123

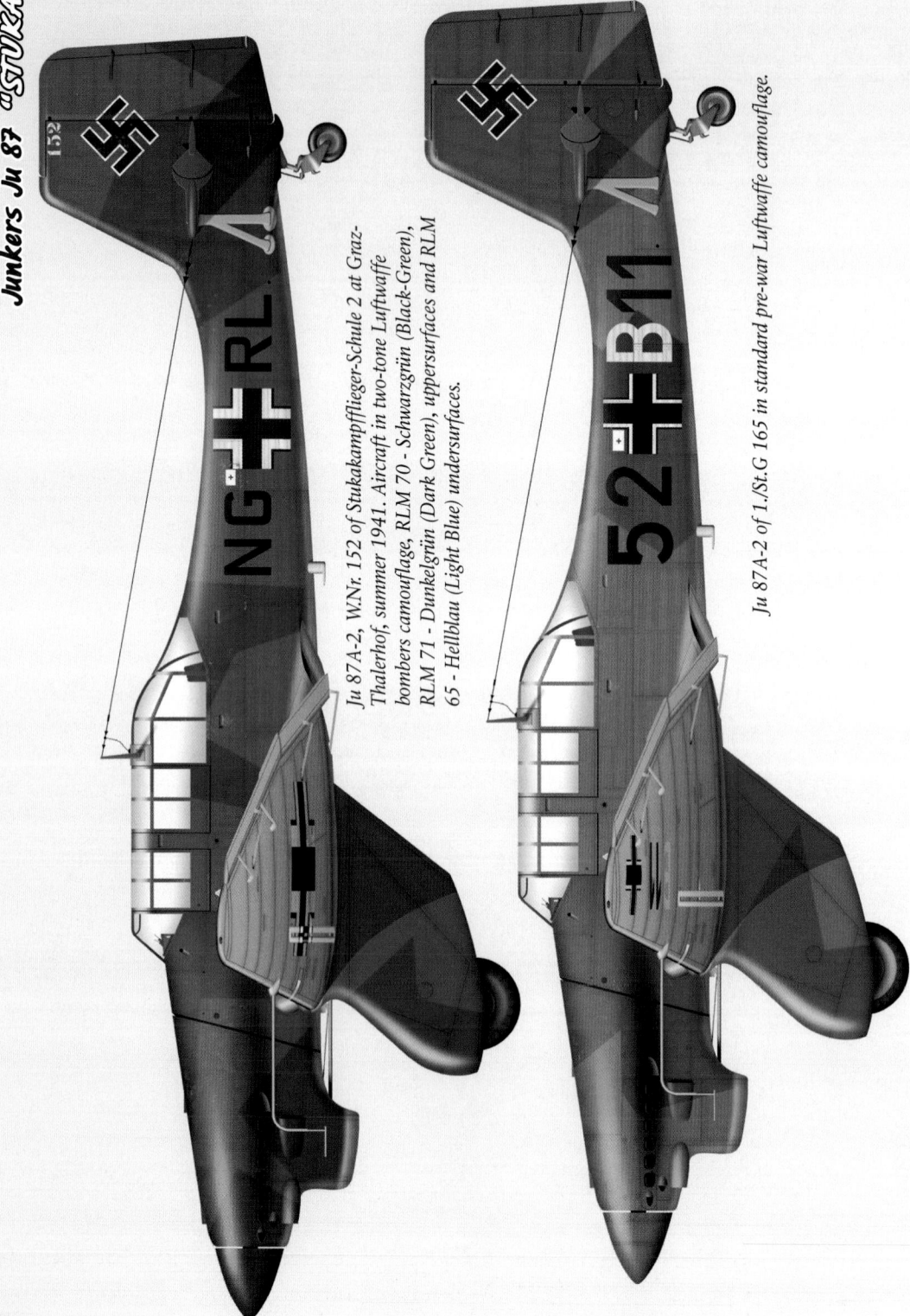

Junkers Ju 87 "STUKA"

Ju 87A-2, W.Nr. 152 of Stukakampfflieger-Schule 2 at Graz-Thalerhof, summer 1941. Aircraft in two-tone Luftwaffe bombers camouflage, RLM 70 - Schwarzgrün (Black-Green), RLM 71 - Dunkelgrün (Dark Green), uppersurfaces and RLM 65 - Hellblau (Light Blue) undersurfaces.

Ju 87A-2 of 1./St.G 165 in standard pre-war Luftwaffe camouflage.

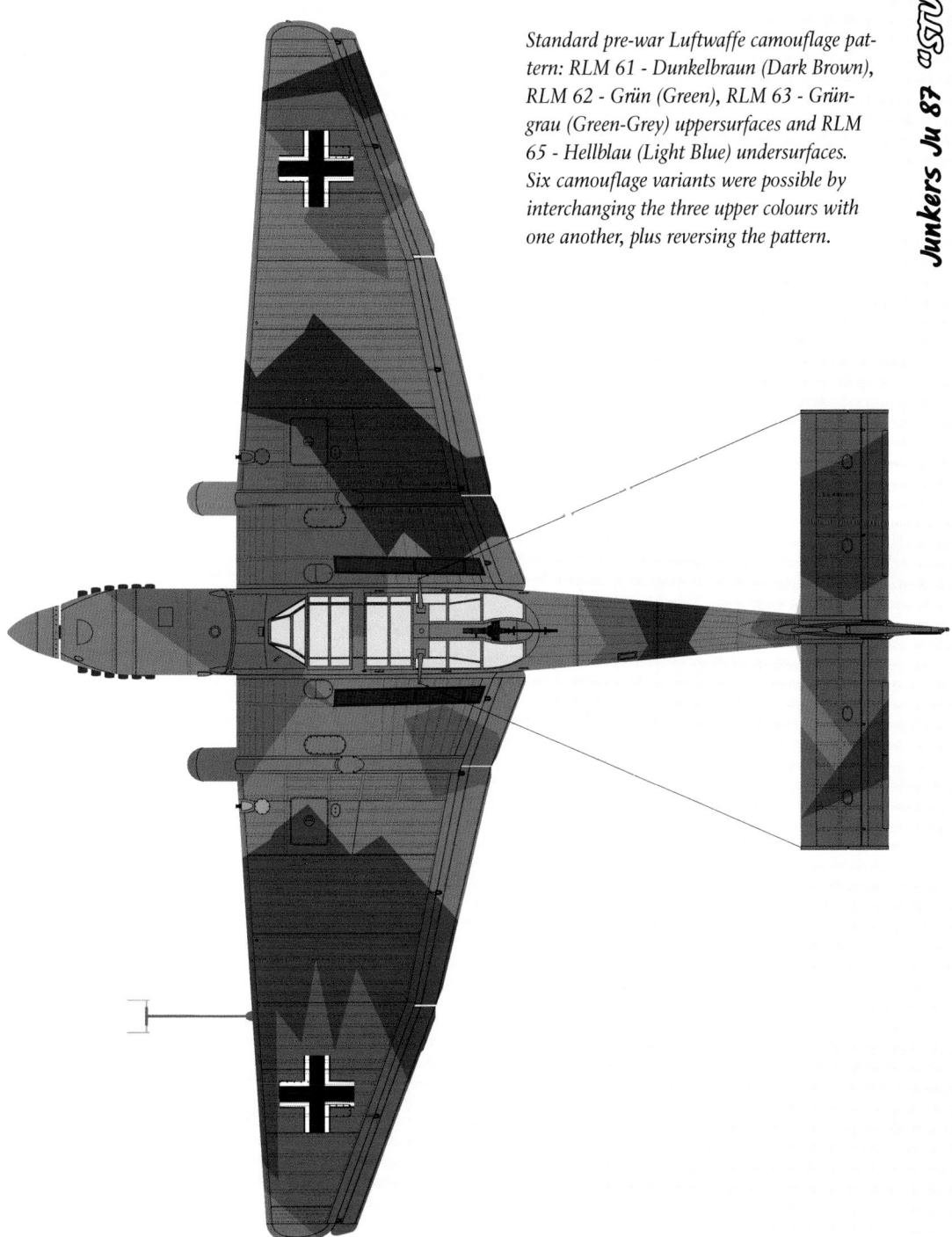

Standard pre-war Luftwaffe camouflage pattern: RLM 61 - Dunkelbraun (Dark Brown), RLM 62 - Grün (Green), RLM 63 - Grüngrau (Green-Grey) uppersurfaces and RLM 65 - Hellblau (Light Blue) undersurfaces. Six camouflage variants were possible by interchanging the three upper colours with one another, plus reversing the pattern.

Junkers Ju 87 "STUKA"

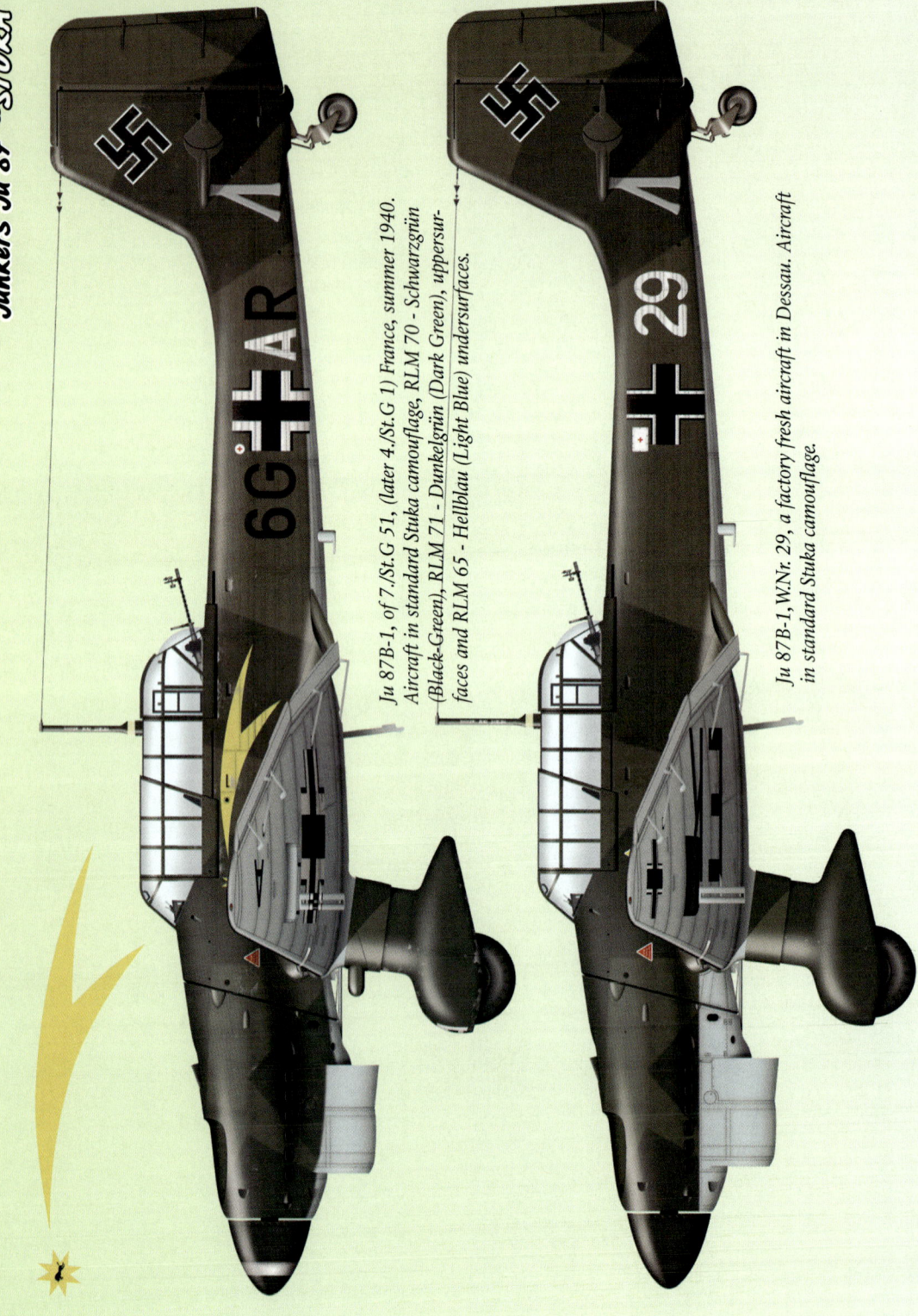

Junkers Ju 87 "STUKA"

Ju 87B-1, of 7./St.G 51, (later 4./St.G 1) France, summer 1940. Aircraft in standard Stuka camouflage, RLM 70 - Schwarzgrün (Black-Green), RLM 71 - Dunkelgrün (Dark Green), uppersurfaces and RLM 65 - Hellblau (Light Blue) undersurfaces.

Ju 87B-1, W.Nr. 29, a factory fresh aircraft in Dessau. Aircraft in standard Stuka camouflage.

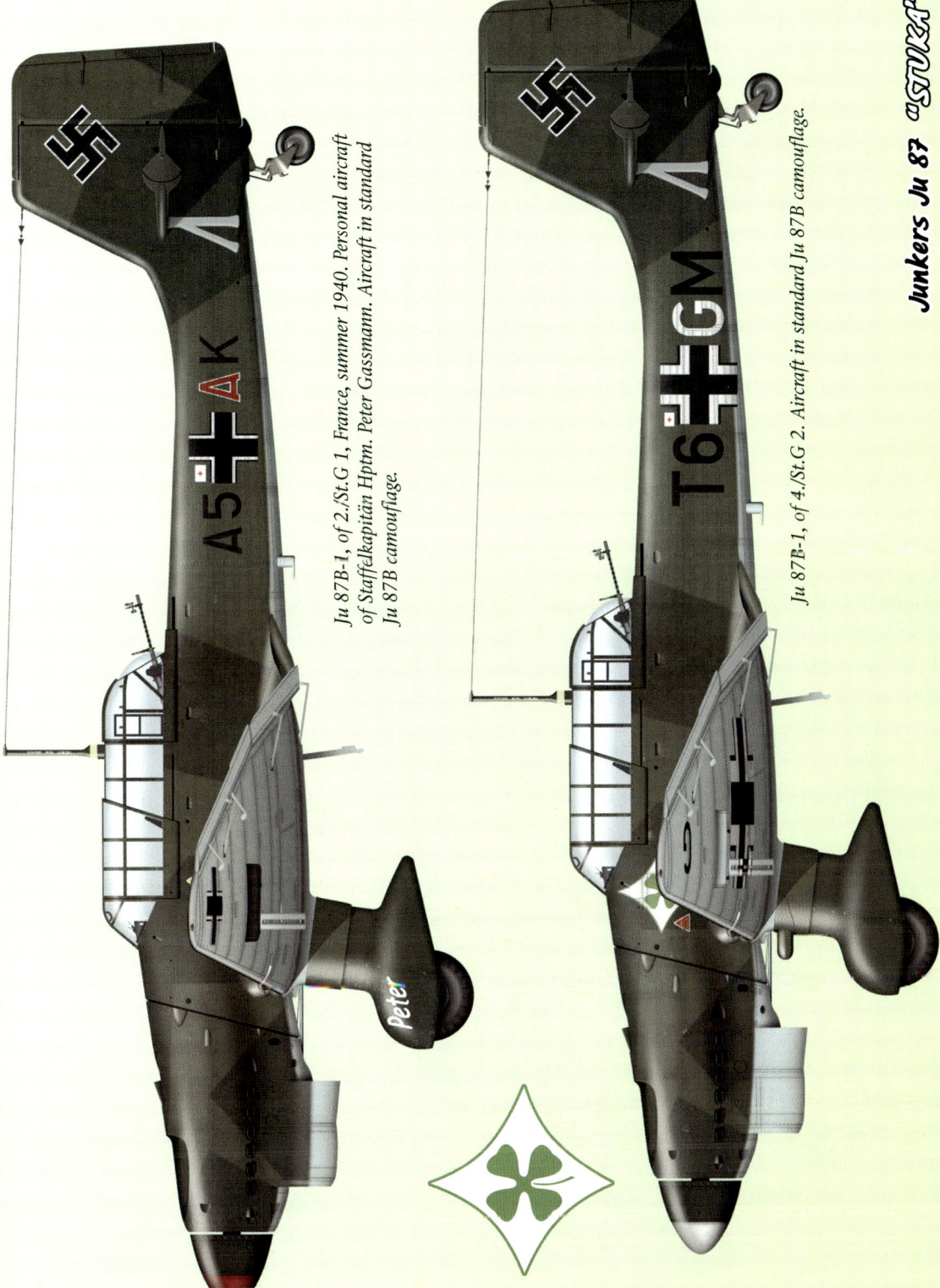

Ju 87B-1, of 2./St.G 1, France, summer 1940. Personal aircraft of Staffelkapitän Hptm. Peter Gassmann. Aircraft in standard Ju 87B camouflage.

Ju 87B-1, of 4./St.G 2. Aircraft in standard Ju 87B camouflage.

Junkers Ju 87 "STUKA"

127

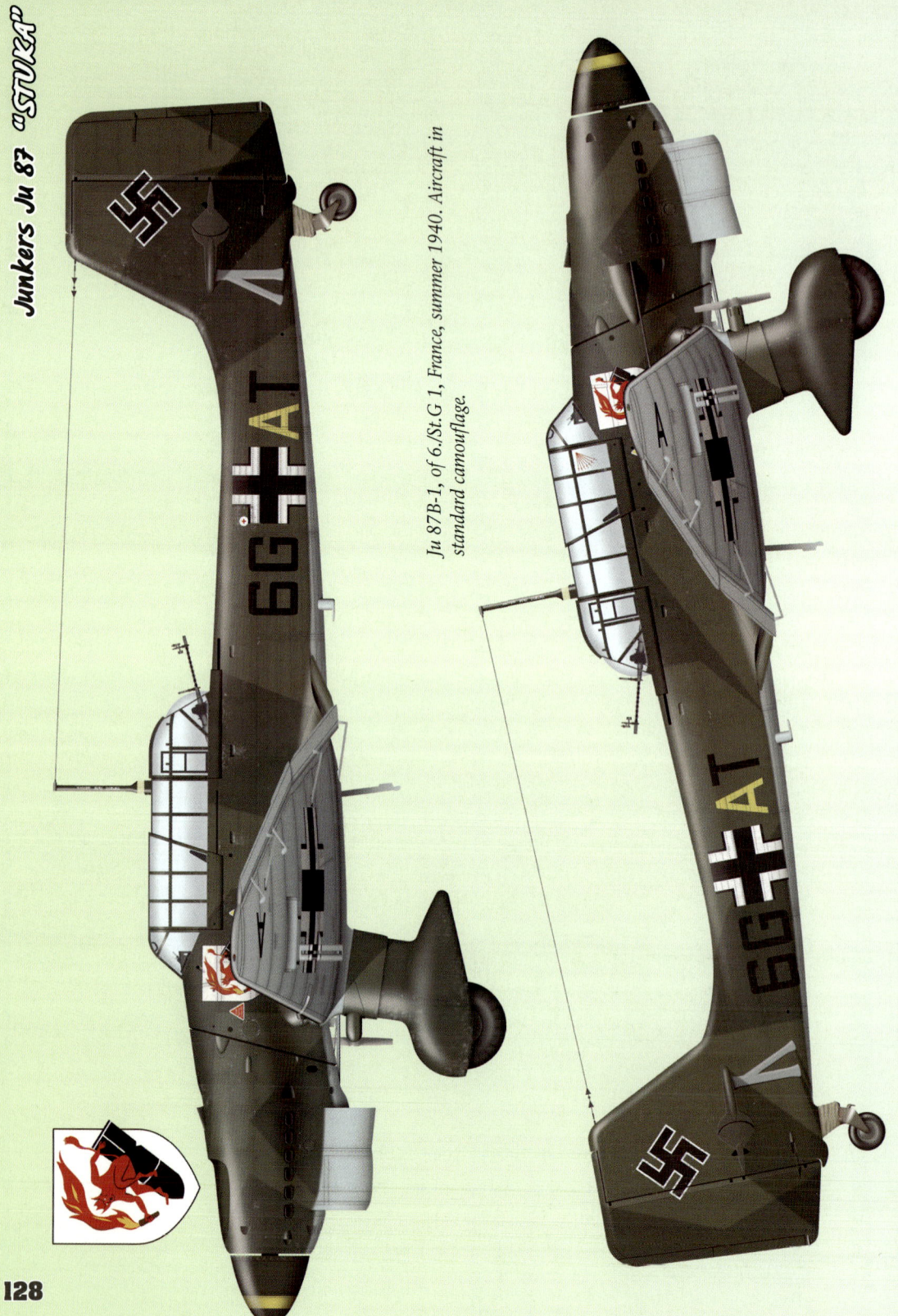

Junkers Ju 87 "STUKA"

Ju 87B-1, of 6./St.G 1, France, summer 1940. Aircraft in standard camouflage.

128

Standard Ju 87B/R upper camouflage pattern: RLM 70 - Schwarzgrün (Black-Green), RLM 71 - Dunkelgrün (Dark Green), uppersurfaces and RLM 65 - Hellblau (Light Blue) undersurfaces.

Junkers Ju 87 "STUKA"

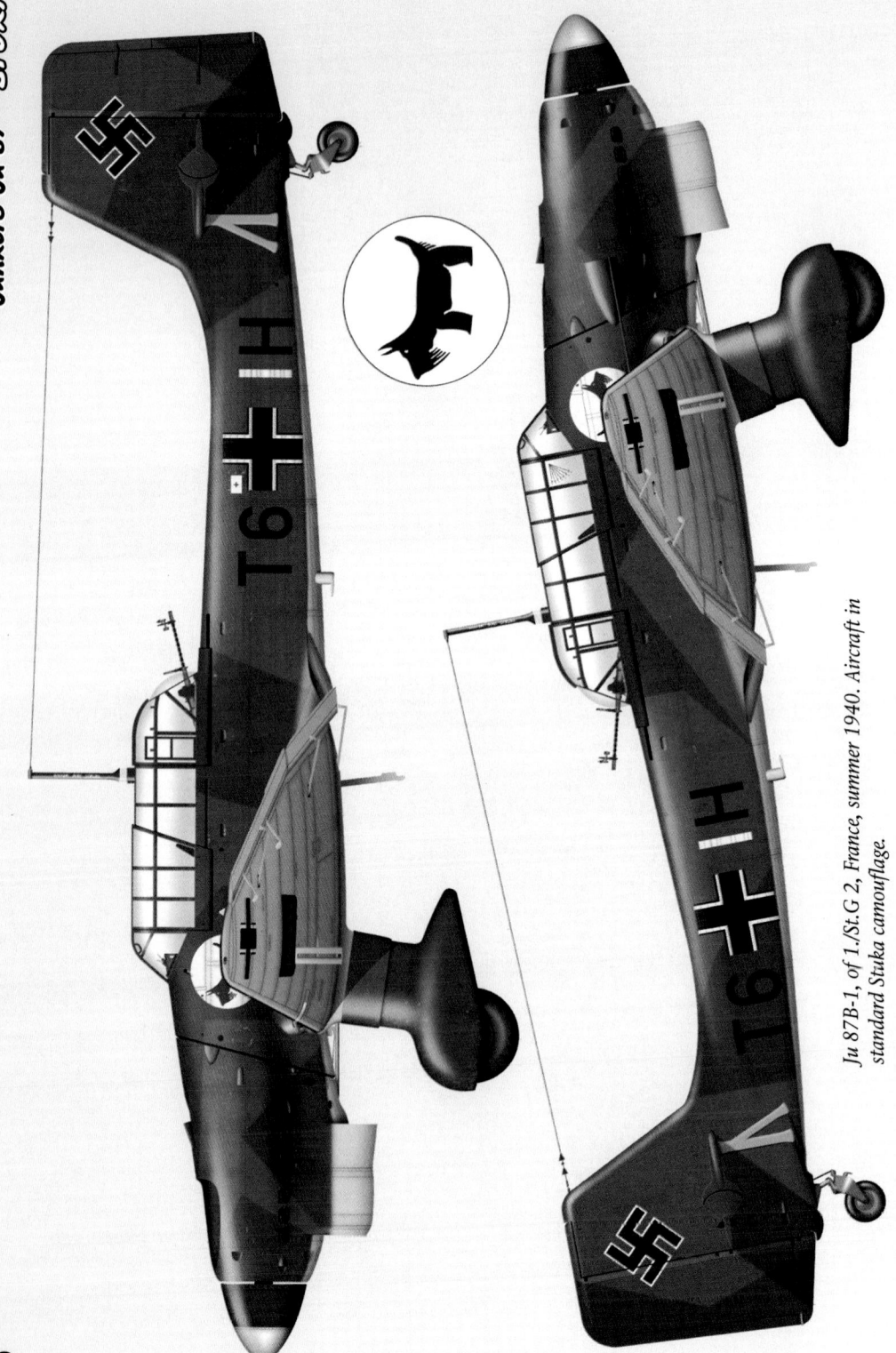

Junkers Ju 87 "STUKA"

Ju 87B-1, of 1./St.G 2, France, summer 1940. Aircraft in standard Stuka camouflage.

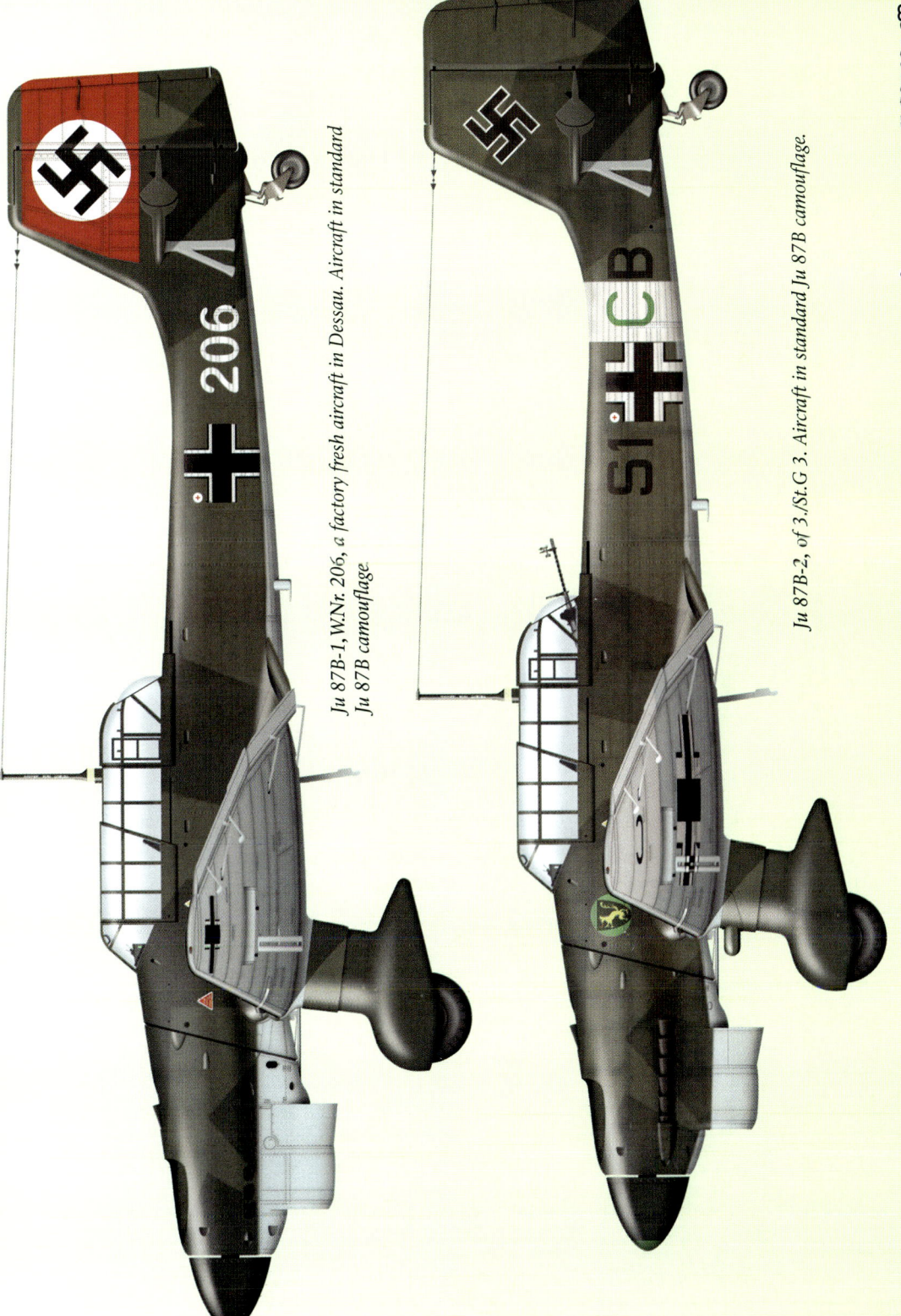

Ju 87B-1, WNr. 206, a factory fresh aircraft in Dessau. Aircraft in standard Ju 87B camouflage.

Ju 87B-2, of 3./St.G 3. Aircraft in standard Ju 87B camouflage.

Junkers Ju 87 "STUKA"

131

Junkers Ju 87 "STUKA"

Ju 87B-2, of 8./St.G 77, Russia, 194. Personal aircraft of Staffelkapitän, Hptm. Gerhard Bauhaus. Aircraft in standard Ju 87B camouflage.

132

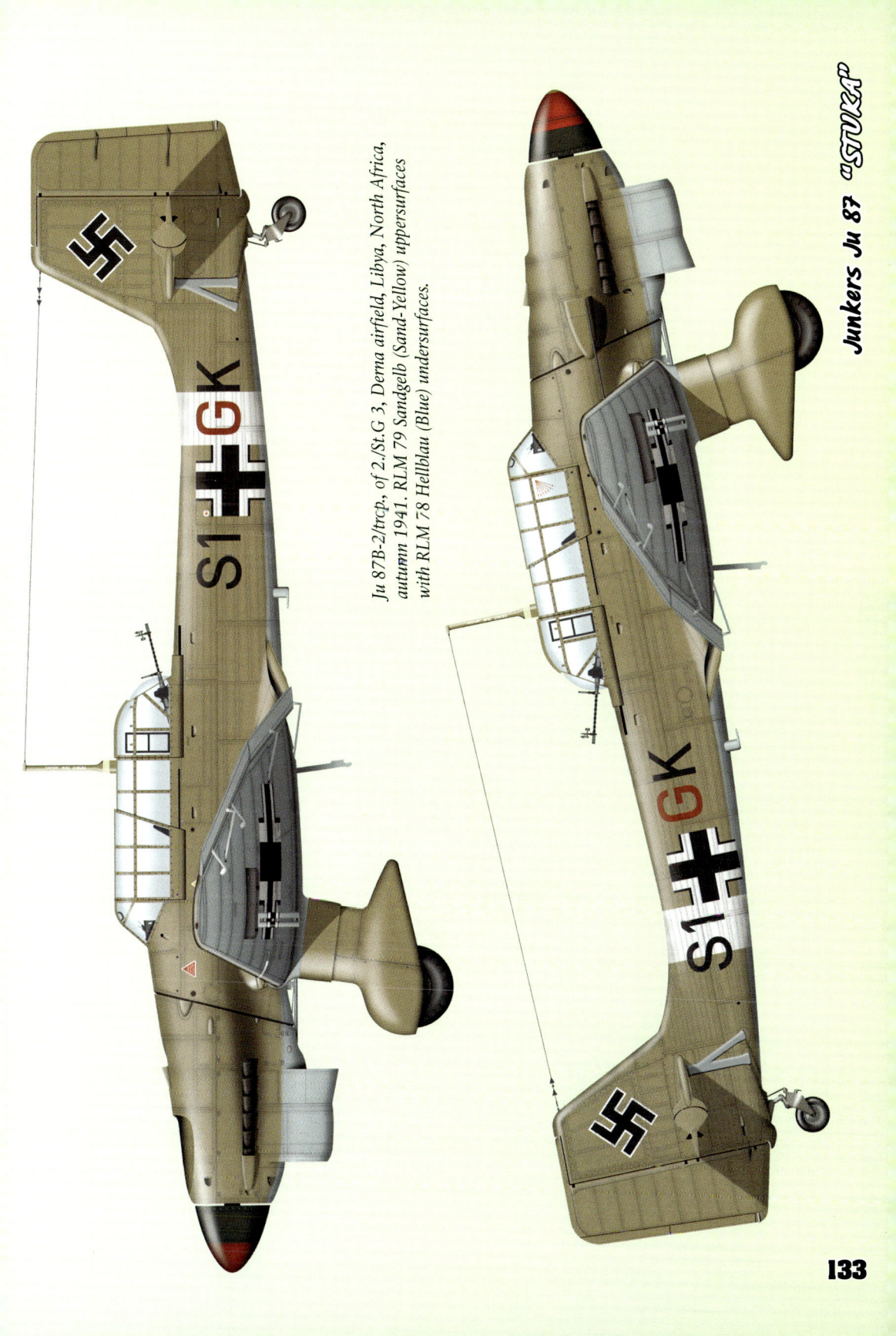

Ju 87B-2/trop, of 2./St.G 3, Derna airfield, Libya, North Africa, autumn 1941. RLM 79 Sandgelb (Sand-Yellow) uppersurfaces with RLM 78 Hellblau (Blue) undersurfaces.

Junkers Ju 87 "STUKA"

Junkers Ju 87 "STUKA"

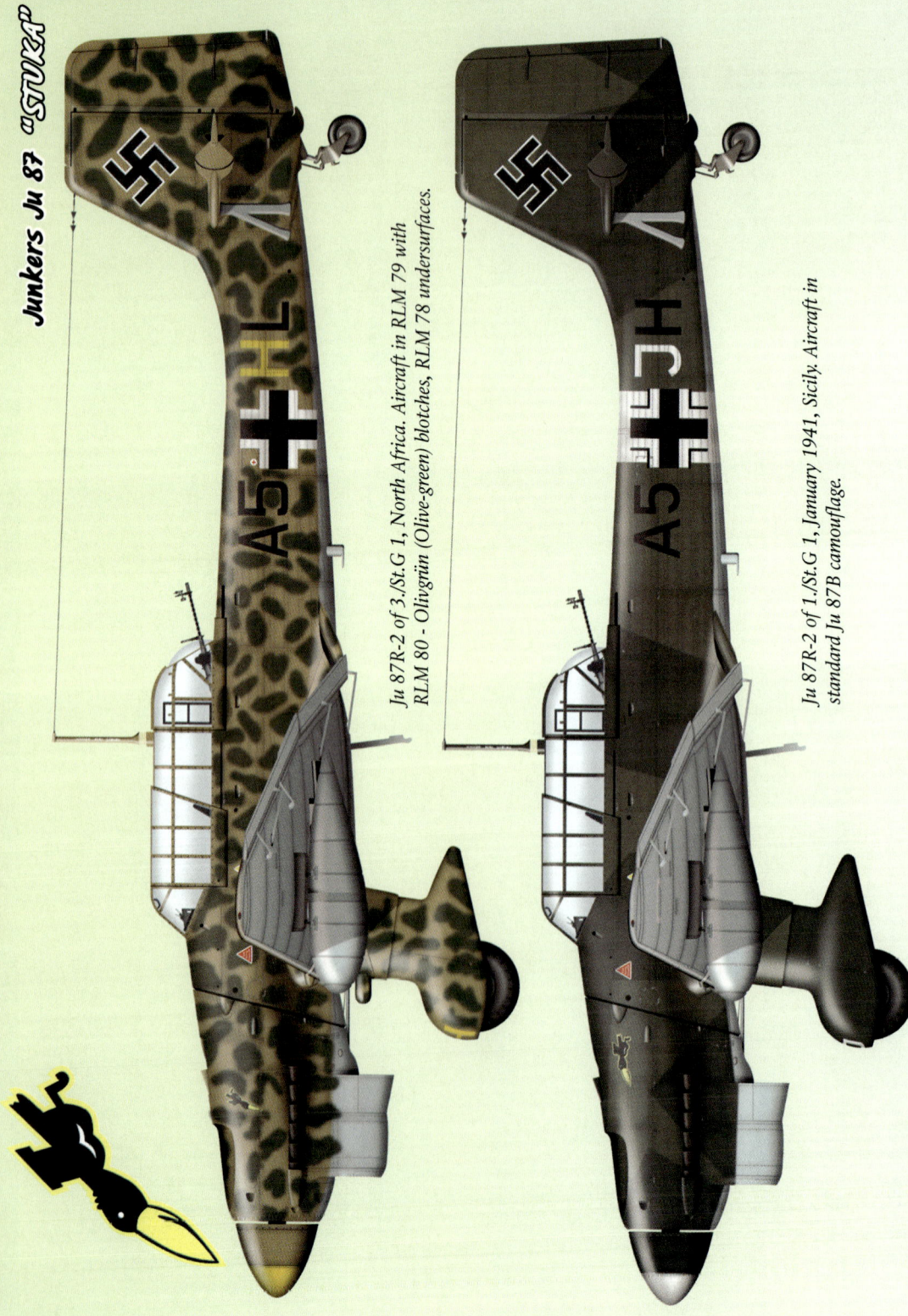

Ju 87R-2 of 3./St.G 1, North Africa. Aircraft in RLM 79 with RLM 80 - Olivgrün (Olive-green) blotches, RLM 78 undersurfaces.

Ju 87R-2 of 1./St.G 1, January 1941, Sicily. Aircraft in standard Ju 87B camouflage.

134

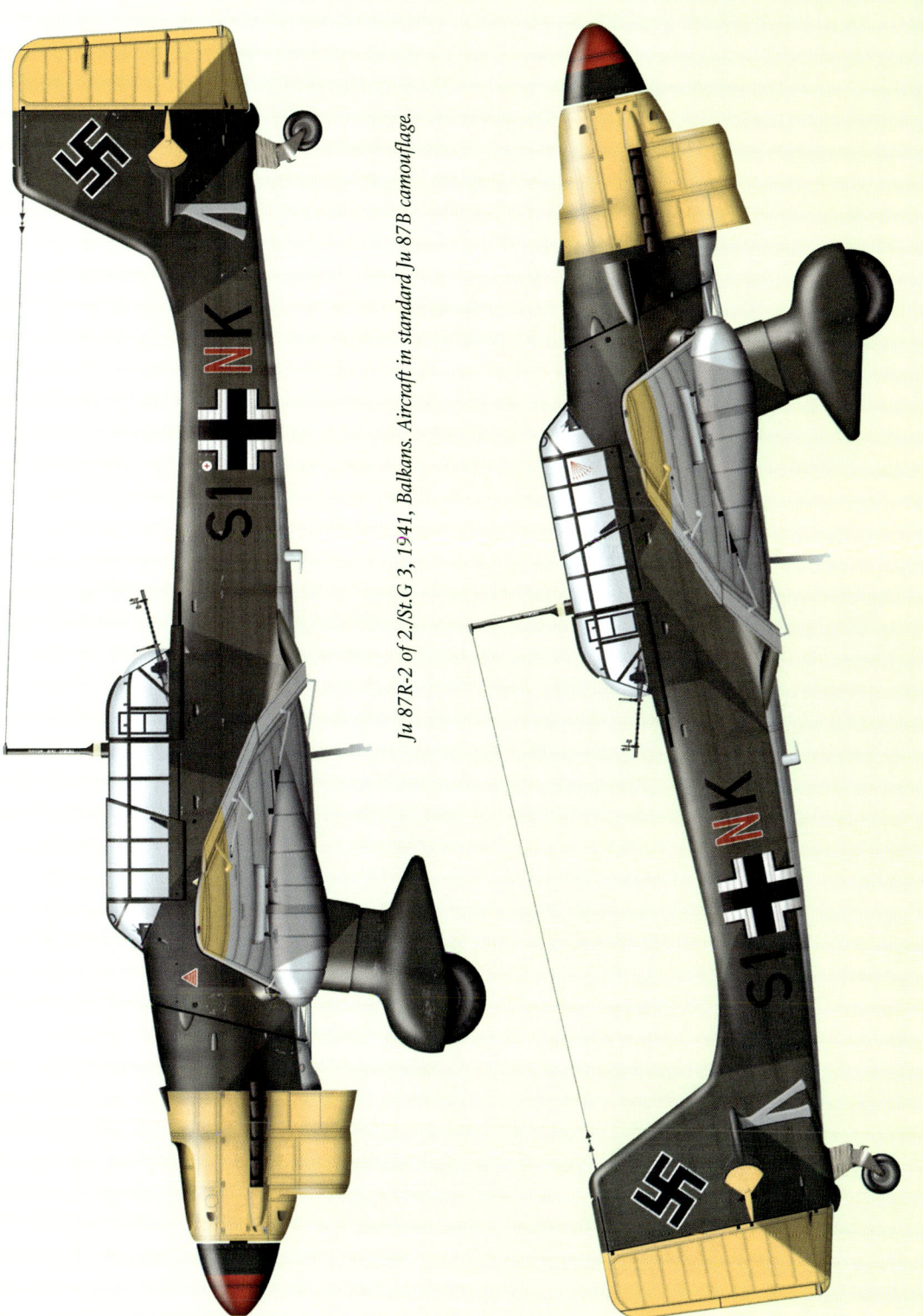

Ju 87R-2 of 2./St.G 3, 1941, Balkans. Aircraft in standard Ju 87B camouflage.

Junkers Ju 87 "STUKA"

135

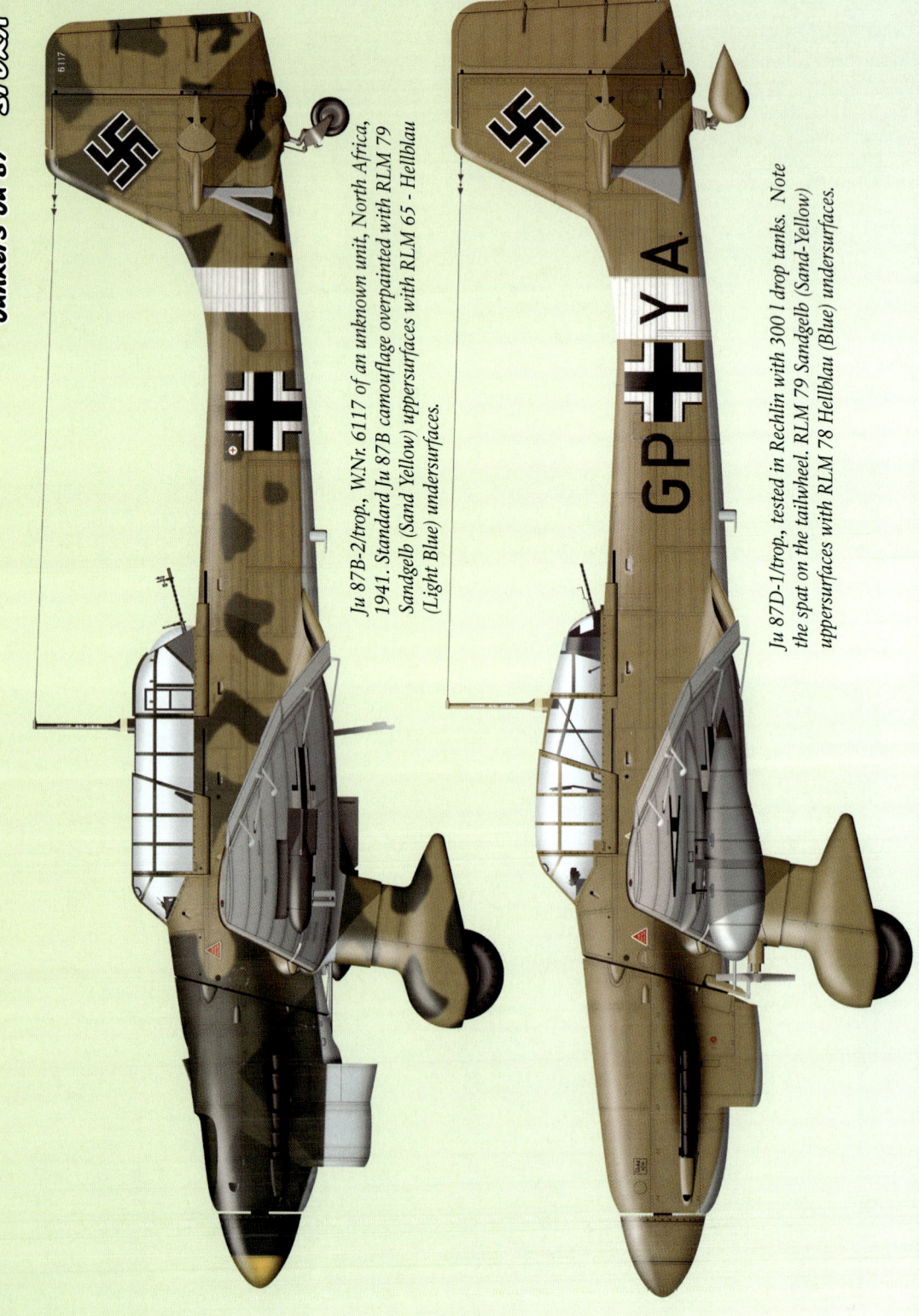

Junkers Ju 87 "STUKA"

Ju 87B-2/trop., W.Nr. 6117 of an unknown unit, North Africa, 1941. Standard Ju 87B camouflage overpainted with RLM 79 Sandgelb (Sand Yellow) uppersurfaces with RLM 65 - Hellblau (Light Blue) undersurfaces.

Ju 87D-1/trop, tested in Rechlin with 300 l drop tanks. Note the spat on the tailwheel. RLM 79 Sandgelb (Sand-Yellow) uppersurfaces with RLM 78 Hellblau (Blue) undersurfaces.

136

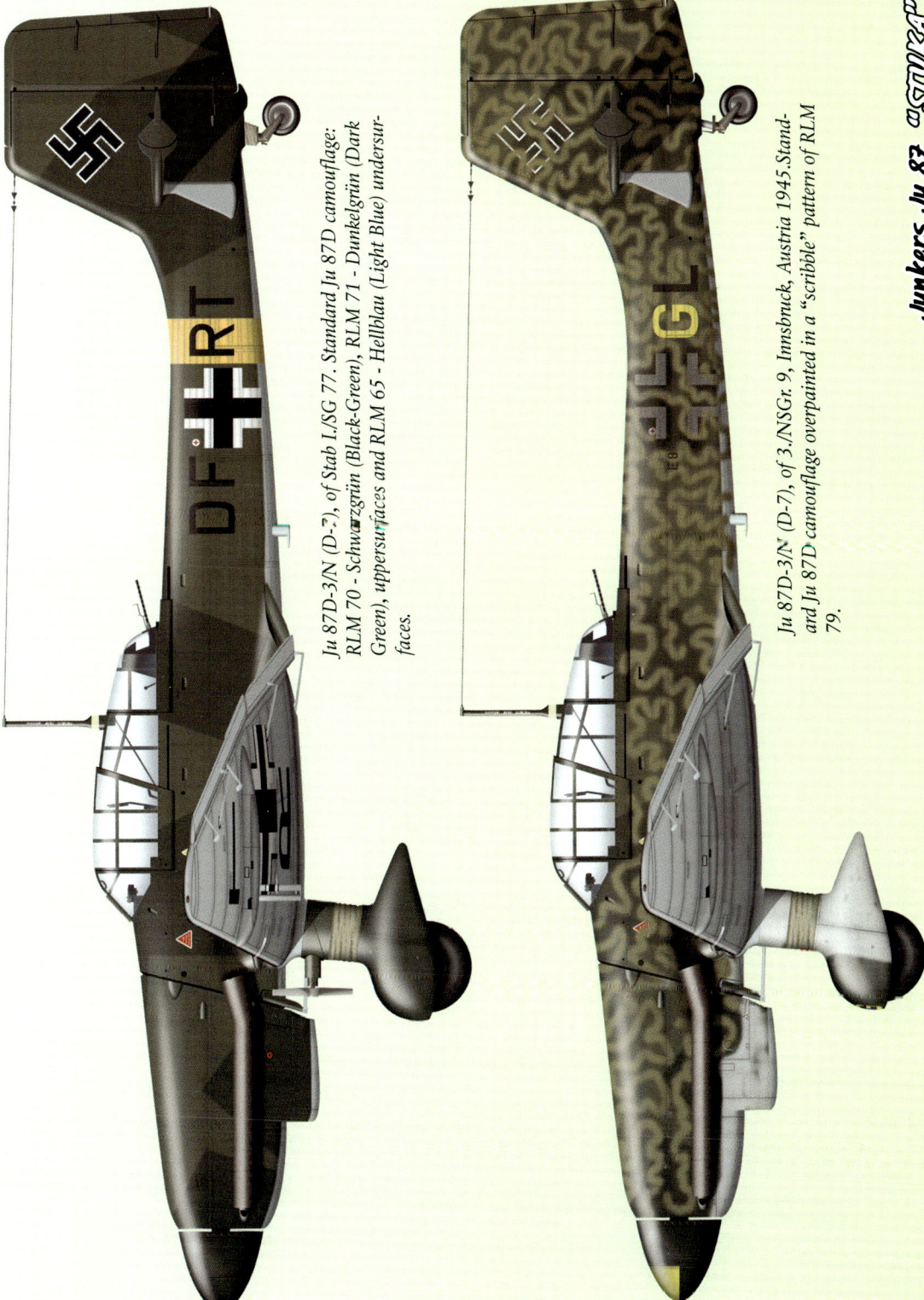

Ju 87D-3/N (D-?), of Stab I./SG 77. Standard Ju 87D camouflage: RLM 70 - Schwarzgrün (Black-Green), RLM 71 - Dunkelgrün (Dark Green), uppersurfaces and RLM 65 - Hellblau (Light Blue) undersurfaces.

Ju 87D-3/N (D-?), of 3./NSGr. 9, Innsbruck, Austria 1945. Standard Ju 87D camouflage overpainted in a "scribble" pattern of RLM 79.

Junkers Ju 87 "STUKA"

137

Junkers Ju 87 "STUKA"

Ju 87D-3 possibly with St.G 77, summer 1943. Aircraft in standard Ju 87D camouflage.

138

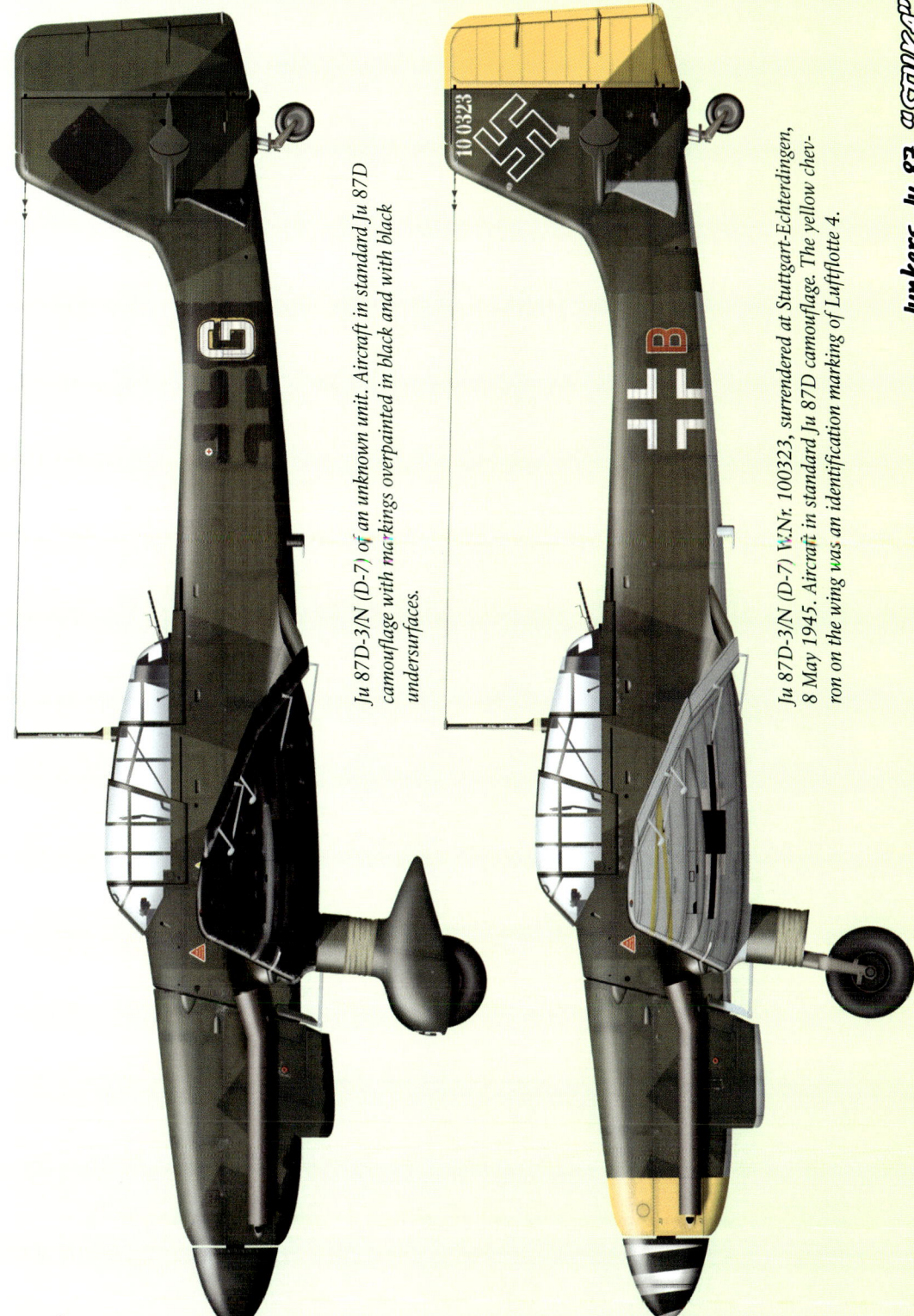

Ju 87D-3/N (D-7) of an unknown unit. Aircraft in standard Ju 87D camouflage with markings overpainted in black and with black undersurfaces.

Ju 87D-3/N (D-7) W.Nr. 100323, surrendered at Stuttgart-Echterdingen, 8 May 1945. Aircraft in standard Ju 87D camouflage. The yellow chevron on the wing was an identification marking of Luftflotte 4.

Junkers Ju 87 "STUKA"

139

Junkers Ju 87 "STUKA"

Ju 87D-3 of Stab. I./SG 77, Eastern Front, summer 1944. Aircraft in standard Ju 87D camouflage.

140

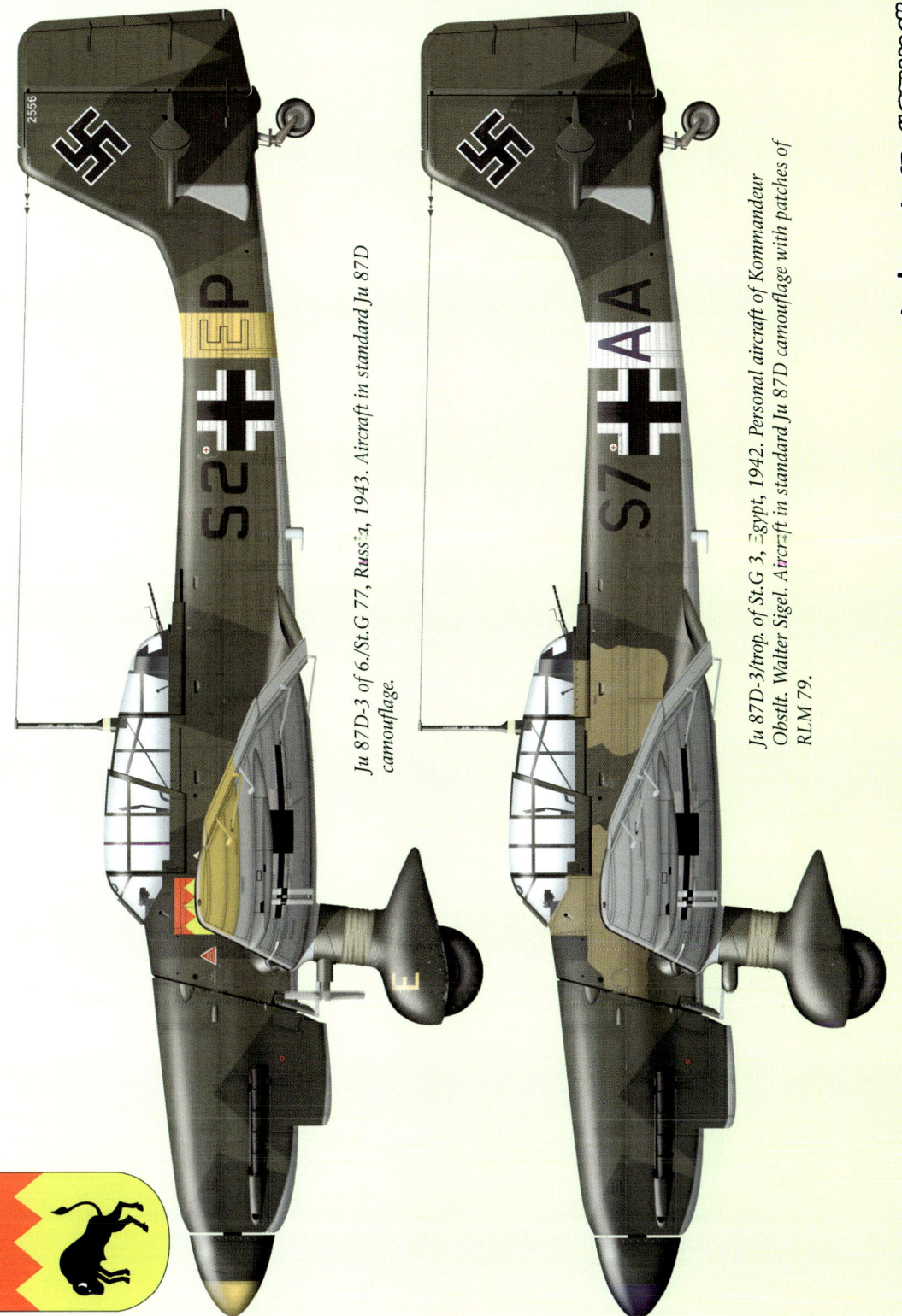

Ju 87D-3 of 6./St.G 77, Russia, 1943. Aircraft in standard Ju 87D camouflage.

Ju 87D-3/trop. of St.G 3, Egypt, 1942. Personal aircraft of Kommandeur Obstlt. Walter Sigel. Aircraft in standard Ju 87D camouflage with patches of RLM 79.

Junkers Ju 87 "STUKA"

141

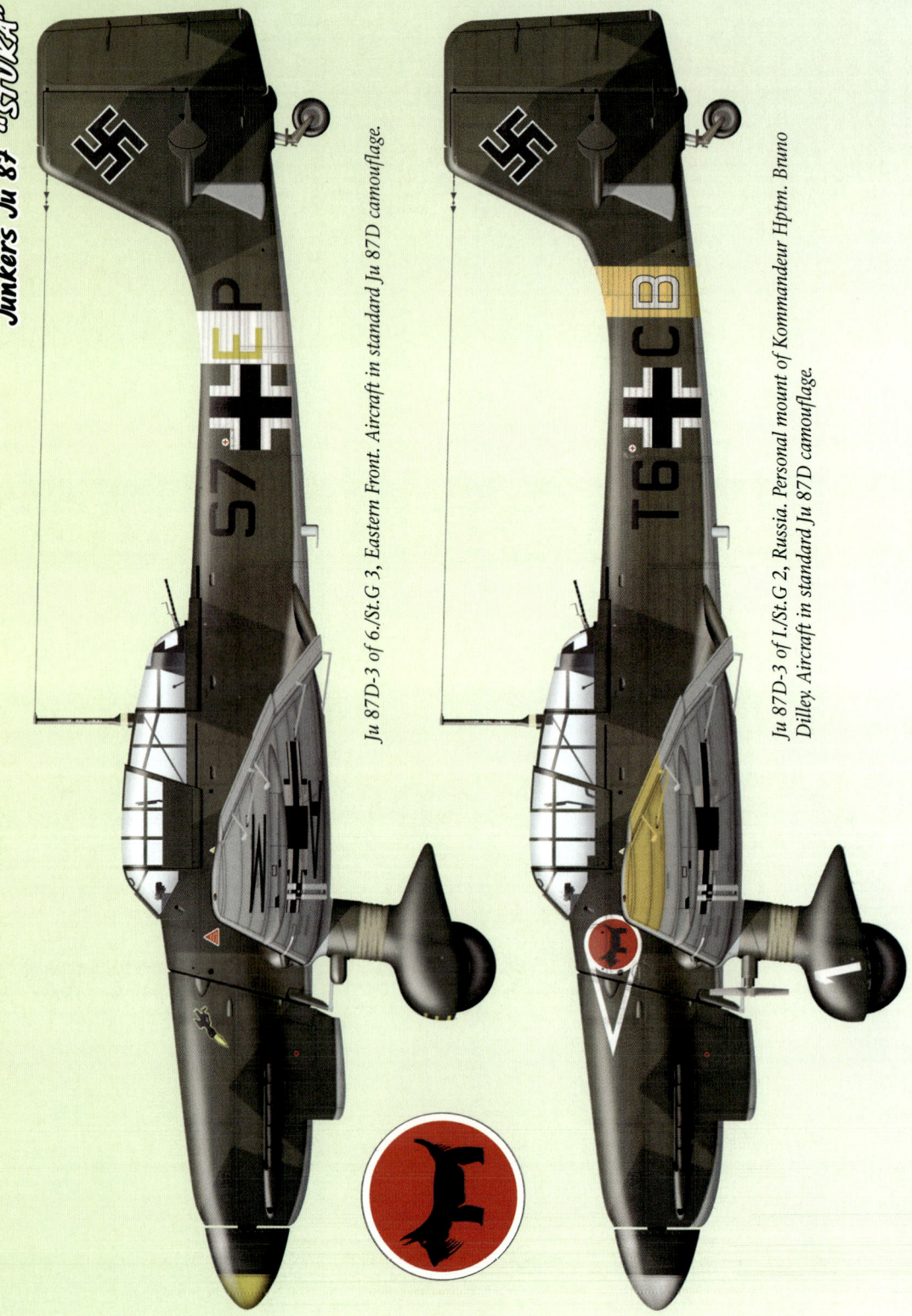

Junkers Ju 87 "STUKA"

Ju 87D-3 of 6./St.G 3, Eastern Front. Aircraft in standard Ju 87D camouflage.

Ju 87D-3 of I./St.G 2, Russia. Personal mount of Kommandeur Hptm. Bruno Dilley. Aircraft in standard Ju 87D camouflage.

142

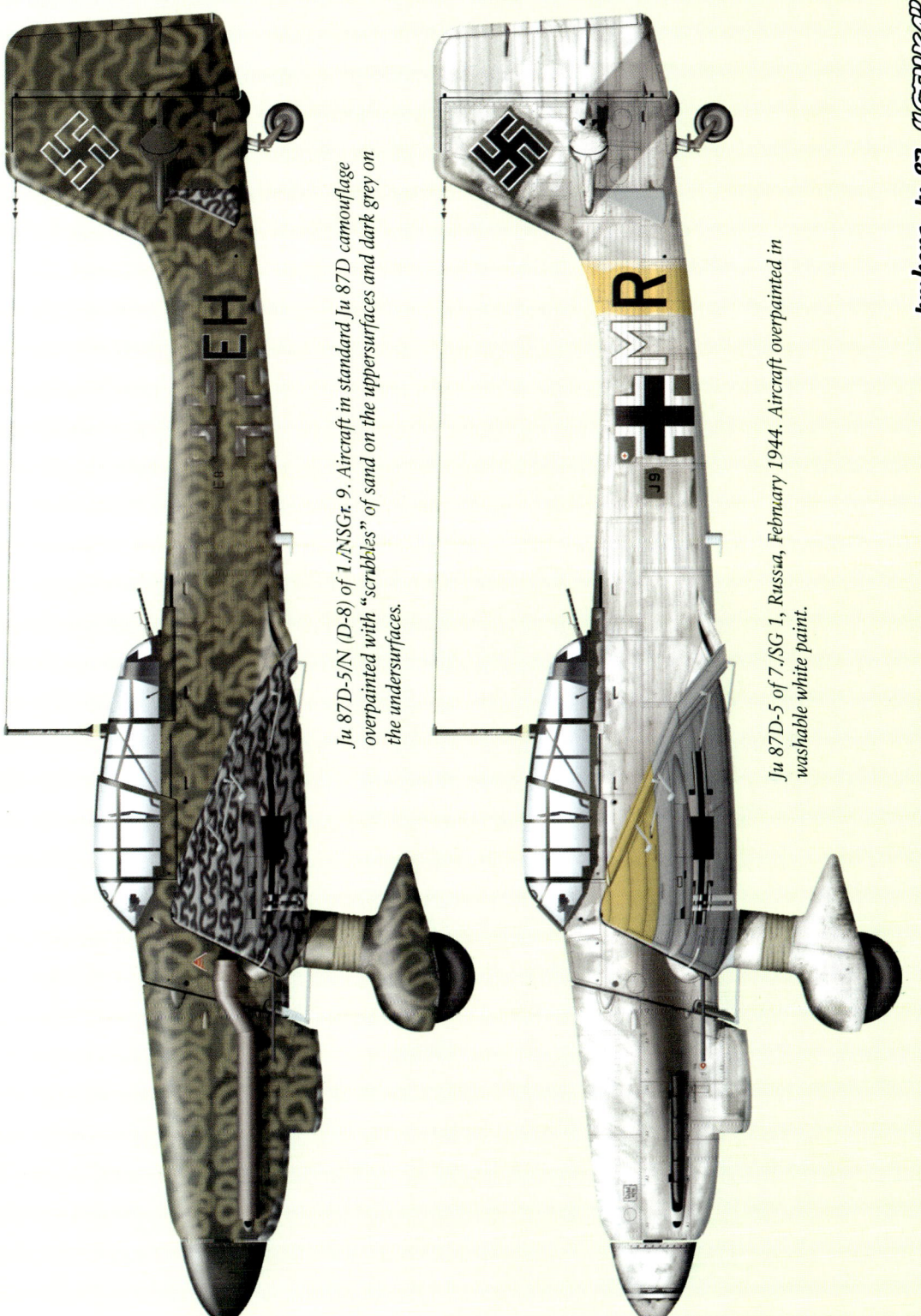

Ju 87D-5/N (D-8) of 1./NSGr. 9. Aircraft in standard Ju 87D camouflage overpainted with "scribbles" of sand on the uppersurfaces and dark grey on the undersurfaces.

Ju 87D-5 of 7./SG 1, Russia, February 1944. Aircraft overpainted in washable white paint.

Junkers Ju 87 "STUKA"

143

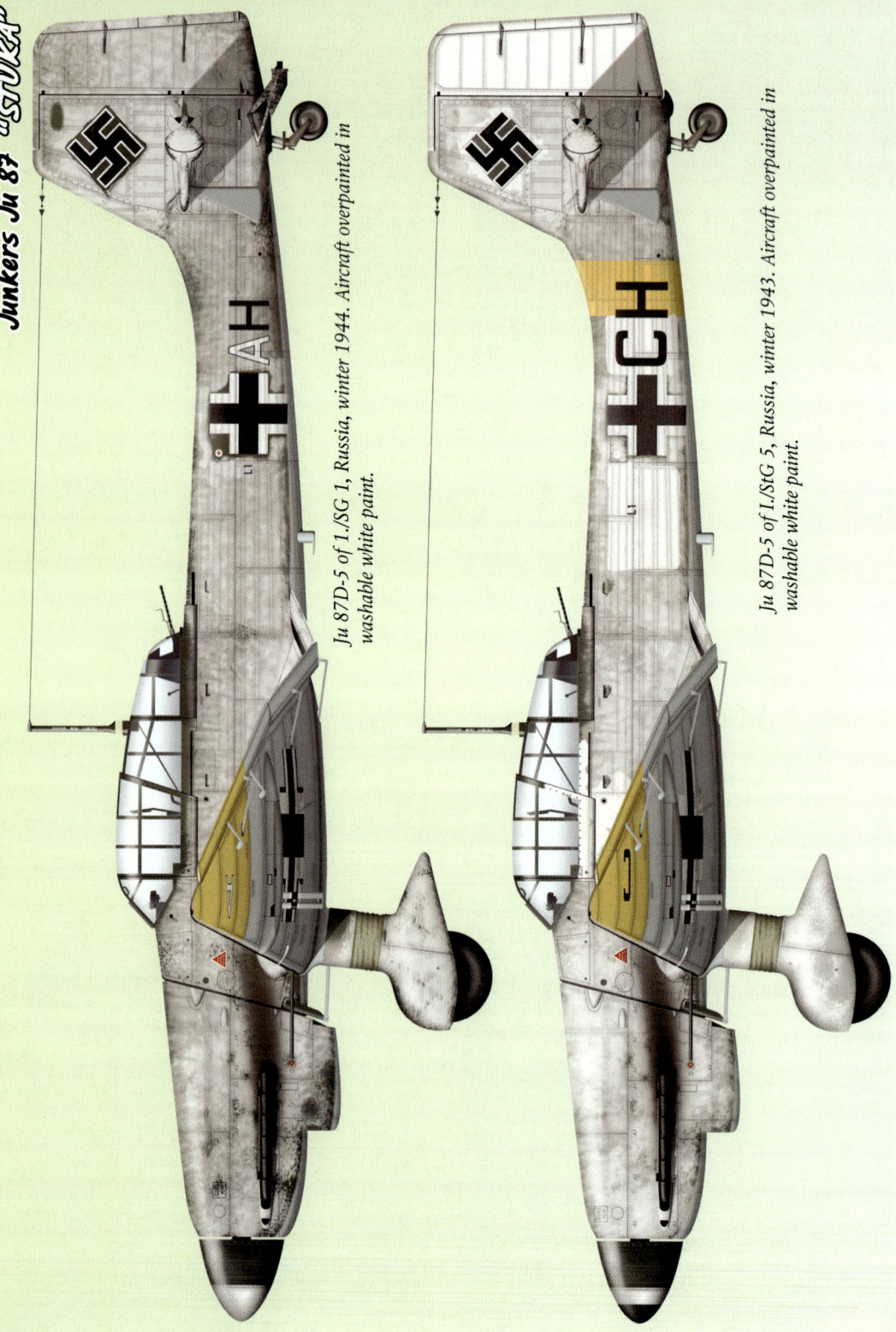

Junkers Ju 87 "STUKA"

Ju 87D-5 of 1./SG 1, Russia, winter 1944. Aircraft overpainted in washable white paint.

Ju 87D-5 of I./StG 5, Russia, winter 1943. Aircraft overpainted in washable white paint.

144

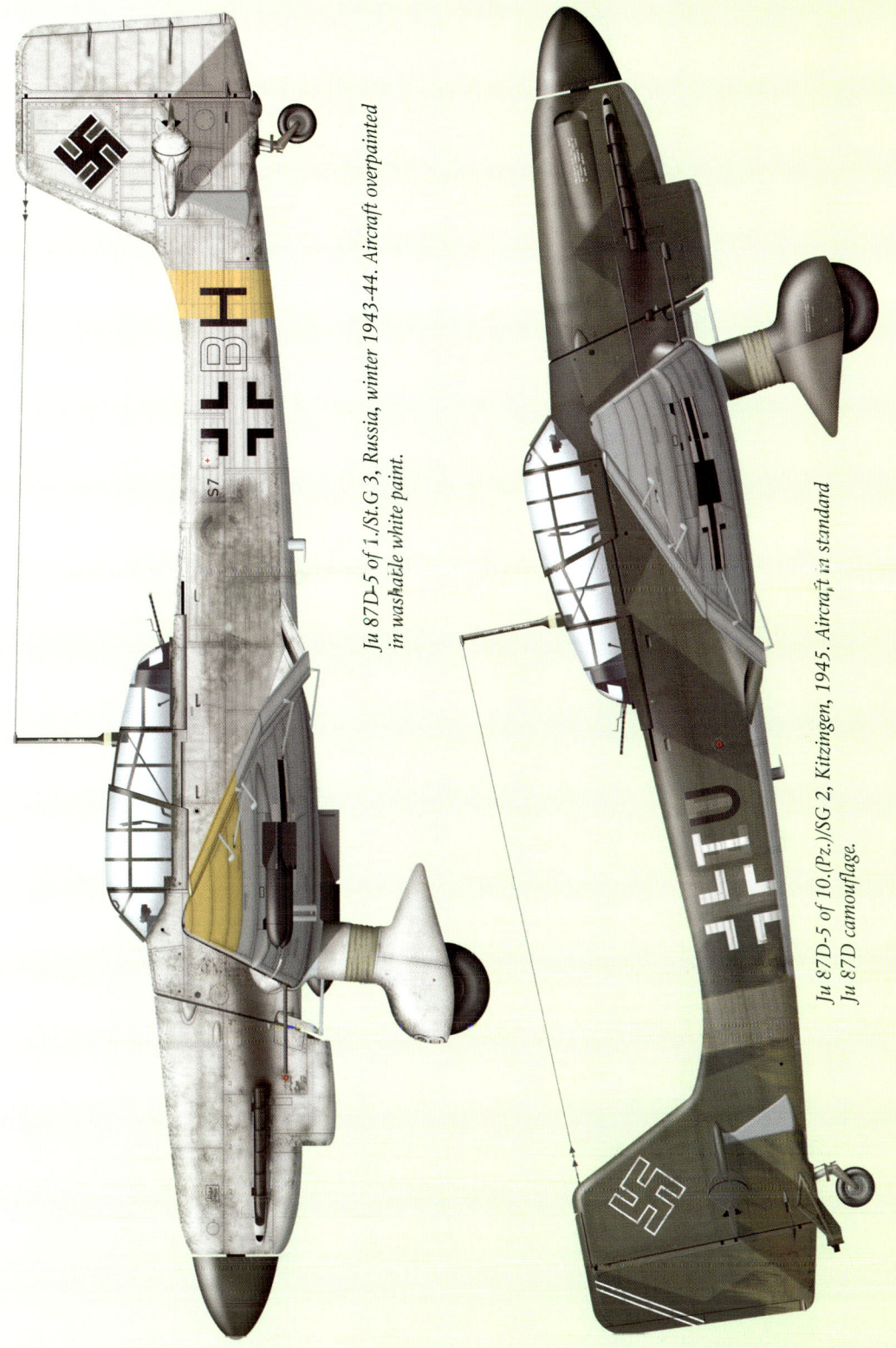

Ju 87D-5 of 1./St.G 3, Russia, winter 1943-44. Aircraft overpainted in washable white paint.

Ju 87D-5 of 10.(Pz.)/SG 2, Kitzingen, 1945. Aircraft in standard Ju 87D camouflage.

Junkers Ju 87 "STUKA"

145

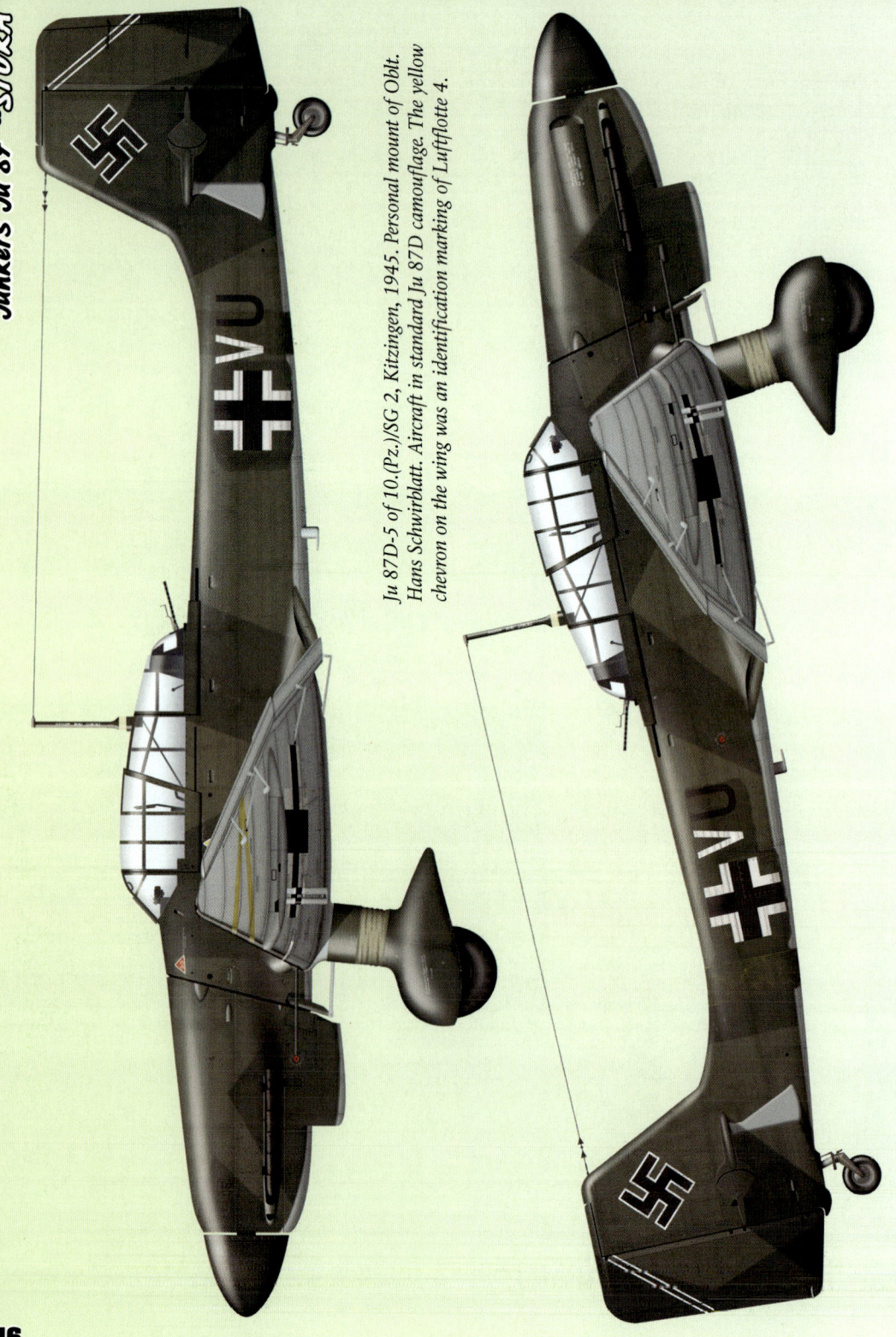

Junkers Ju 87 "STUKA"

Ju 87D-5 of 10.(Pz.)/SG 2, Kitzingen, 1945. Personal mount of Oblt. Hans Schwirblatt. Aircraft in standard Ju 87D camouflage. The yellow chevron on the wing was an identification marking of Luftflotte 4.

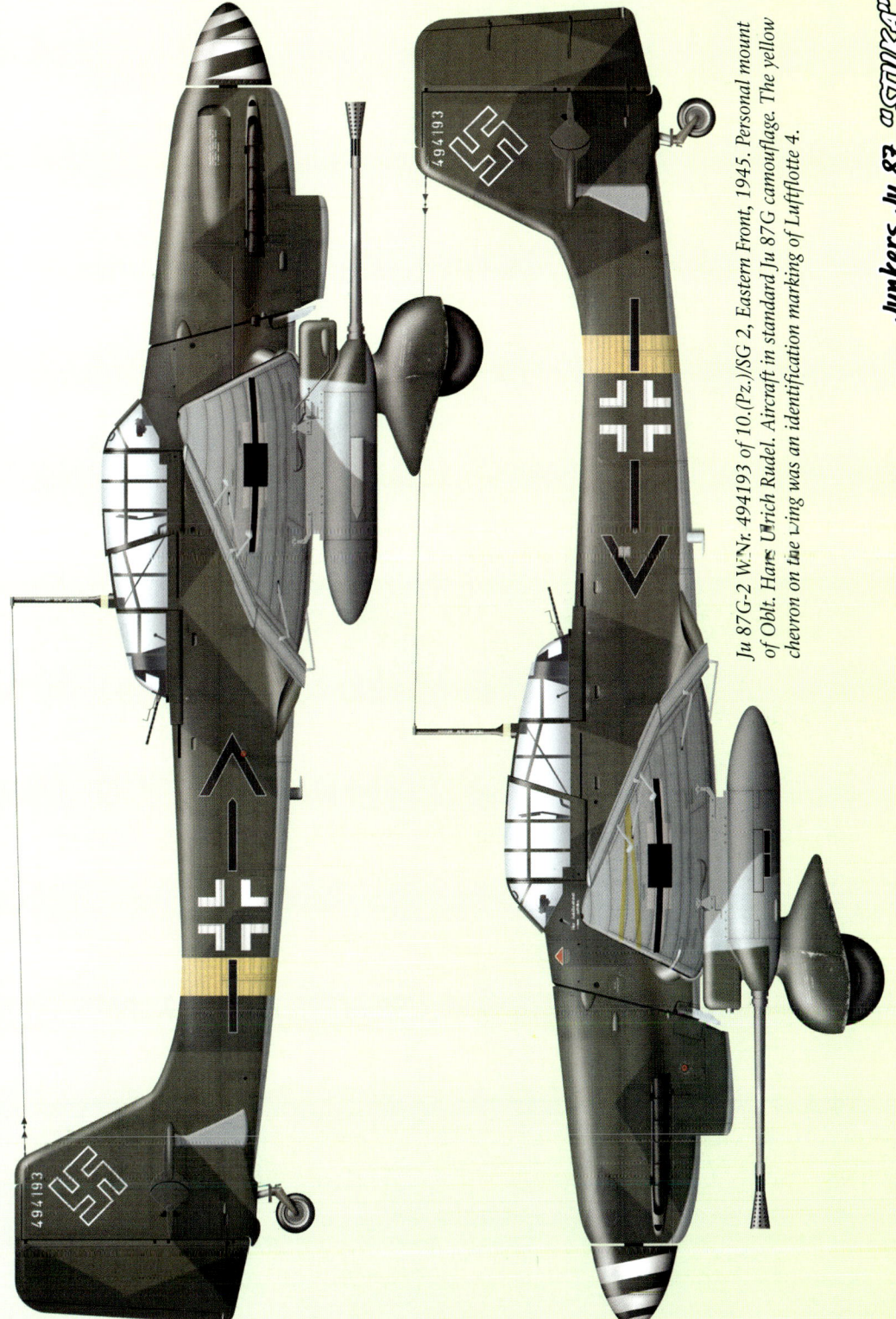

Ju 87G-2 W.Nr. 494193 of 10.(Pz.)/SG 2, Eastern Front, 1945. Personal mount of Obl. Hans Ulrich Rudel. Aircraft in standard Ju 87G camouflage. The yellow chevron on the wing was an identification marking of Luftflotte 4.

Junkers Ju 87 "STUKA"

Junkers Ju 87 "STUKA"

Standard Ju 87D/G upper camouflage pattern: RLM 70 - Schwarzgrün (Black-Green), RLM 71 - Dunkelgrün (Dark Green), uppersurfaces and RLM 65 - Hellblau (Light Blue) undersurfaces.

148

Ju 87G-2 of III./SG 2, Hungary, September, 1944. Personal mount of Oberst Hans Ulrich Rudel. Aircraft in standard Ju 87G camouflage.

Junkers Ju 87 "STUKA"

149

Junkers Ju 87 "STUKA"

Ju 87G-2 W.Nr. 494110 of 10.(Pz.)/SG 2, Kitzingen, 1945. Hans Ulrich Rudel escaped in this aircraft to the American part of the front. Aircraft in standard Ju 87G camouflage. The yellow chevron on the wing was an indentification marking of Luftflotte 4.

Ju 87G-2 W.Nr. 494200 of an unknown unit, Plzen, May, Aircraft in standard Ju 87G camouflage.

150

Ju 87G-2 W.Nr. 491216 of 10.(Pz.)/SG 2, Eastern Front, 1945. Aircraft in standard Ju 87G camouflage.

Ju 87G-2 W.Nr. 494221 of 10.(Pz.)/SG 2, Eastern Front, 1945. Aircraft in standard Ju 87G camouflage.

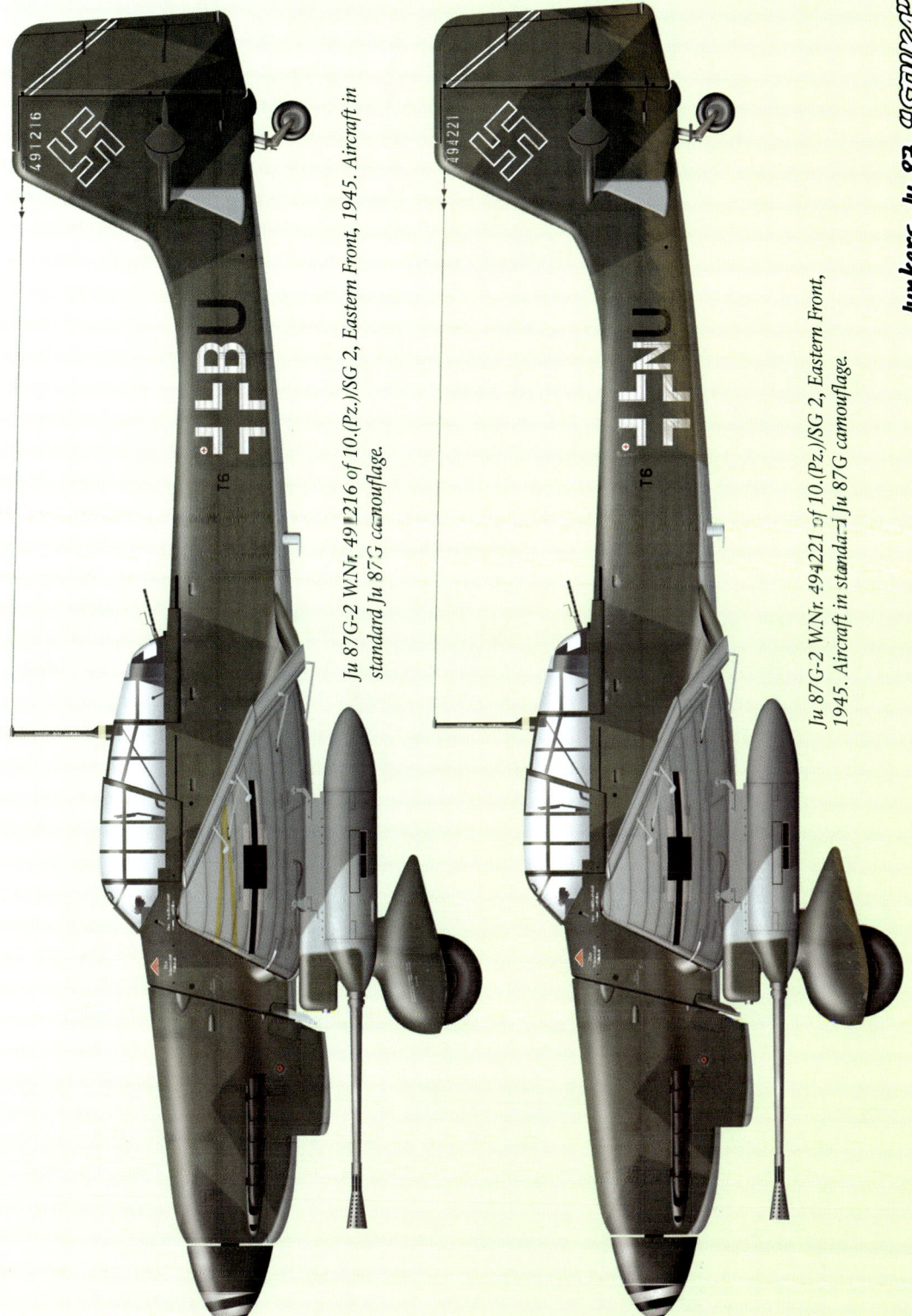

Junkers Ju 87 "STUKA"

151

Bibliography

Bilý, Miroslav. Junkers Ju 87 A Stuka. MBI, 1991

Bilý, Miroslav. Junkers Ju 87 Stuka. MBI/Sagita, 1992

Brown, Captain Eric. Wings of the Luftwaffe. Pilot Press (1977, 1979) and by Airlife (1987, 1993)

Dressel, Joachim. Stuka! Arms and Armour Press, 1989

Filley, Brian. Ju 87 Stuka in Action. Squadron/Signal Publications, 1986

Griehl, Manfred. Junkers Ju 87 Stuka, Airdoc 005. 2006

Jane's Fighting Aircraft of World War II. Bracken Books, 1989

Junkers Ju 87 D/G Stuka, Aero Detail 11. Dai Nippon Kaiga Co. Ltd. 1994

Ketley, Barry & Mark Rolfe, Luftwaffe Emblems 1939-1945. Hikoki Publications, 1998

Longyard, William H. Who's Who in Aviation History. Airlife, 1994

Merrick, K.A. Luftwaffe Camouflage & Markings 1935-45, Vol 1. Kookaburra Technical Publications Pty. Ltd, 1973

Michulec, Robert. Uwaga Stukas!, Część 1. Armagedon, 2000

Murawski, Marek J. Ju 87 Stuka Monografie Lotnicze 19. AJ-Press. 1994

Murawski, Marek J. Junkers Ju 87 Vol. I. Kagero, 2005

Murawski, Marek J. Junkers Ju 87 Vol. II. Kagero, 2006

Murawski, Marek J. Junkers Ju 87 Vol. III. Kagero, 2006

Philpott, Bryan. The Encyclopedia of German Military Aircraft. Arms and Armour Press, 1980.

Shirer, William L. The Rise & Fall of The Third Reich. Heineman Ltd., and Secker and Warburg Ltd., 1969

Smith, Peter C. Dive Bombers in Action. Blanford Press, 1988

Smith, Peter C. Luftwaffe Ju 87 Stuka Dive-bomber Units: 1942-1945 v. 2 (Luftwaffe Colours), Classic Publications, 2006

Smith, Peter C. Dive Bomber! An illustrated history. Moorland publishing, 1982

Smith, Peter C. Stuka: Luftwaffe Ju 87 Dive-Bomber Units 1939-1941 v.2 (Luftwaffe Colours), Classic Publications, 2006

Smith, Peter C. Junkers Ju 87 Stuka. Crowood, 1998

Taylor, Michael J. H. The Aerospace Chronology. Tri-Service Press, 1989

Weal, John. Junkers Ju 87: Stukageschwader Mediterranean and North Africa. Osprey CombatAircraft, Osprey, 1998